Wendy's Way

from Cornish Village to World Stage

Wendy Eathorne

The Choir Press

First published in the United Kingdom in 2026 by The Choir Press

ISBN 978-1-78963-574-4

Acknowledgements

To my wonderful daughter Alice, her husband Laurence and talented granddaughters Arabella and Ottilie.

To Michael and Alice for preparing the photographs and most of all supporting me and listening.

To Rachel for guiding me throughout publishing which I have so much enjoyed.

Contents

CHAPTER ONE

At Home

❋

I was born in Cornwall in September 1939, just after the start of the Second World War. I had two wonderful parents, Daddy, Henry a builder, and Mummy, Olga, a teacher, both born under the sign of Leo, and my clever sister, Harriet, born in September a year before me.

After cycling to Wendron about eight miles every day from Four Lanes, Mummy taught at Wendron Primary School. There she met Canon Gilbert Hunter Doble, who was at the time Vicar of Wendron Parish Church. He spent twenty years at the church, was a scholar of Exeter College, Oxford and graduated in modern history. Mummy never stopped talking about him and how he had educated her in so many aspects of religion and the history of Cornwall. Mummy could quote avidly from the Bible to us children and to a religious sect who would visit at Christmas time to promote their beliefs.

The Methodist Chapel in Four Lane where we spent Sundays

Daddy, a Freemason and a quiet practical man, was strong and influential with strict ideas about our upbringing. He wouldn't allow me to paint, that being a man's job, but he spoilt my sister and me enormously. We received brand new bicycles at Christmas, mine a Triumph! He constantly advised what we should or shouldn't do, maybe because he drove, as project manager, a van full of lustful men to work every day. To my dismay, during the very busy summer months many of the village youngsters would work as waiters in St Ives but, after Daddy's quick negative answer to my request to join them, he assured me that if I needed the extra cash, he would give it to me. Of course, that was not the point and I was very sad about it.

My father built this bungalow where I was born and lived before going to the Royal Academy of Music

Daddy worked for Thomas and Co, a building company, where he was eventually offered the job of director. He refused because he didn't want to spend time travelling away from the family. He died in 1969 at the age of 64, having worked from the age of 13. It was as the eldest child that he had joined his father in Wales, working to help support his siblings. Not being invited to live with his father he experienced a very unhappy time there. Consequently, neither my grandfather nor Daddy is mentioned in the 1921 census in Cornwall but only my grandmother, Harriet Ellen Eathorne, whom I never met, and her eight children. She died in her forties in the arms of her daughter, my Auntie Bessie, who lived to be a hundred.

Harriet and I in our Sunday best dresses

At home Harriet spent most of her time reading, but when Daddy came home from work my job was to look after him and get his cigarettes from the next-door shop if he needed them. I jumped over the granite wall at the front of the bungalow in order to get there faster. Daddy was so happy to display our front granite wall of the bungalow in the village and I believe we had one of the first bathrooms there. Such a luxury! The bungalow was built by Daddy, helped by his brothers, who were also tradesmen. Da, Mummy's father, was a foreman in the Crofty Mine near Four Lanes. Warm and kind, Da sat in his armchair after work, very much the patriarch, eating my grandmother's delicious chips. Very sadly he died at sixty from pneumoconiosis, a mining disease. He was one of seventeen children! My grandmother Nana's father went to South Africa to work during the depression. He sent her back loads of money but did not return. Nana supplied lots of food for the village folk and never passed a beggar without being generous. Nana died at seventy.

*Mummy and Daddy in the garden on a
sunny afternoon*

*My grandparents Nana and Da back
from work as a miner*

*My Nana when she was in
her thirties*

Mummy the teacher standing on the right

A disappointment for Mummy was when Lady Vivien of St Michael's Mount, after hearing Mummy, a soprano, sing at one of the trio concerts that she performed around the county, offered her financial help to study at one of the Royal Music Colleges. Da was not happy and thought the idea of my mother going to London was something he could not possibly consider. At that time just to travel two and a half miles to Redruth from Four Lanes needed a horse and cart. Since Four Lanes is 700 feet above sea level the horses going up the hill from Redruth back to Four Lanes required the passengers to get out so that the horse could manage the hill. One could see Da's reasoning and maybe a little bit of pride, also possibly the very reason why Mummy was keen for me to go to a music college!

Mummy tells me that when I was in my pram a large dog came to say hello. Mummy, rather frightened by this, shooed him away. This resulted in me being frightened of dogs for the rest of my life. Da, my grandfather, had a dog called Queenie who always followed him. I walked with him one day into the village and the dog followed.

I said to Da, "That bloody dog is coming again!" He immediately went to see Mummy to ask her where I learnt such language. I don't remember her reaction to it but expect that I was duly chastised.

My sister Harriet and I went to Four Lanes Primary School just outside the village and walked there and back with Mummy. During those early years of the war, we were spoilt with sweets and such like by the American soldiers stationed in the village and I was chosen by them as their favourite, so I'm told. I believe we children were not the only ones spoilt by the soldiers! Mummy taught at the school for a while when needed and I, at the age of four, accompanied my five-year-old sister, Harriet, to school which meant Mummy was free to help out. I was apparently a bit of a nuisance, always wanting to join in before other children had a chance. I was warned every day to be quiet.

I remember one day Mummy announcing, "Wendy, listen. It's the Prime Minister's speech. THE WAR IS OVER!" The sirens had stopped.

Our time as children continued and life was based mainly around the Methodist Church or at school. Harriet and I went to the Methodist Church in the village three times a Sunday, to the morning service, Sunday School in the afternoon and joined by Mummy and Daddy all in our best attire for the evening service, where they were members of the Chapel choir. Occasionally there were concerts after the evening service which always went on far too long.

When a tenor in the choir once sang, "To love *myself* more dearly every day," instead of *"someone"*, Mummy muttered, "That's typical of him!" We could hardly contain our laughter!

On occasions when Uncle Max, the organist, was on holiday I would play the hymns for the evening service minus the pedals, which from the high stool I could not reach. Mummy read avidly and had all the Daphne Du Maurier books, which Harriet dipped into. I was overjoyed when an amateur dramatic society put on some plays based on Daphne Du Maurier's novels for a whole week in the village church Sunday School Hall. I went every night and loved my first experience of theatre. My first experience of professional concerts was every year on Good Friday in the Camborne Wesley Methodist Church when we attended a concert of Handel's *Messiah*. Harriet and I thought it was rather long and we were warned not to move. Daddy assured me that proof that my singing career was really successful would be to be invited to Camborne Wesley to sing *Messiah*. The comment was perhaps understandable since every year the solo parts were sung by professional singers such as Bruce Boyce, Olive Groves and Henry Cummings. They were all still teachers at the Royal Academy of Music when I was a student there.

D.M. Thomas, the British novelist, poet, playwright and translator, was born in the village, Carn Bray, just over the hill from Four Lanes, and is best known for his novel, *The White Hotel*. Don dated my friend, Maureen, who lived next door to us in the village and of course my family met him and had many boozy drinks with him. Mummy bought his first set of poems. She read them and then hid them, thinking that they were rather too 'spicy' for our delicate ears. My partner, Michael, and I still had Zoom times with him and Angela, his wife, during the ghastly pandemic time. He lived in Cornwall but sadly died in 2023. Michael and Don were never happier than when they had a bottle of brandy between them.

There was of course the Harvest Festival where everyone joined together to decorate the Chapel with vegetables, fruit and such like. It was lavish and wonderful! A stage was erected for the children's special concert. My singing debut was when I was three with guess what? *Twinkle twinkle little star!* A standing ovation! We all wore beautiful new

D.M. Thomas

dresses. Apparently, according to Mummy I could sing before I could speak. This was maybe because Mummy sang to us all the time. As a baby my sleeping habit was irritating. I would go to bed, sleep and then wake up again. The music

> *"In Mansions of Glory and endless delight*
> *I'll ever adore thee in heaven so bright."*

was sung over and over again until I slept. When we were a bit older Mummy arranged little concerts in chapels around Cornwall where Harriet and I sang duets she chose for us.

"Wendy, will you make up a descant or alto line, please?" she would say.

We were taught the piano by a blind man who visited the village by bus each week and we would collect him from the Square about a hundred metres away. He was so kind and placed his hand on ours to check we were not playing with flat fingers.

I went to Chapel for five years without missing any services, for which I was given a copy of Handel's *Messiah*. Daddy being the eldest of nine children meant that we had numerous cousins and enjoyed parties on farms many times in the year, one special one in the snow. Things I

My lovely kind and fun Aunties who gave wonderful parties

remember are Auntie Bessie Brown's miniature jellies with fruit and Cornish cream, Auntie Bessie Kemp's tiny perfumed sweets and the view of an incubator of tiny chicks at her farm. There was cuddly Auntie Annie and uncle John Eathorne – two portions of fish and chips in Redruth on Fridays!

"Lovely on my lap, isn't it dear?" as Auntie Annie squeezed me against her ample bosom. Another Auntie Annie Eathorne had a hide and seek house where we just couldn't find our hidden cousins, Janice and Vivien, anywhere. They were holding on to the rafters above the staircase! As adults we visited our eighty-odd-year-old blue-haired Auntie Bessie, Mummy's sister, in a home in Camborne where she introduced me to her friends.

"This is Wendy, excuse her hair!" to which I replied, "But this is as my hair is."

"No, it isn't, dear!"

I remember most of all the Christmas parties at Eathorne house in the village. Aunt Nell, our step-grandmother, hosted wonderful celebrations for all the family. There would be three table settings, limited Methodist drinks of course, children's displays of the Aunties' Sunday best outfits, hats and coats (horrors!) and a choir in the evening of Merit's Carols, conducted by the amusing Uncle Alex, even though Uncle Wilfred, conductor of the Four Lanes Male Voice choir, was present. All great fun!

On weekends in the summer Harriet and I were taken to beautiful beaches at St Ives or Carbis Bay in a car which Daddy had built, stopping at St Day for splits to make banana sandwiches to eat on the beach. Other weekends to Falmouth and hot pasties en route. There is a steep hill from the main road to the beach in Carbis Bay. We would have a wonderful time on the beach but then there was the problem of getting the car up the hill to the main road home. Mummy, Harriet and I waited at the bottom of the hill while Daddy revved the engine of BU0 608 to get up the hill. Daddy could get to the top of the hill provided there were no restrictions but quite often he would have to stop, take the car back down the hill and try again. Fun for Harriet and me! On the route home we would stop at Camborne Square where in a restaurant on the first floor we would have high tea. The building is now a popular Wetherspoons restaurant, I believe. Finishing the journey we had a sing-song, Daddy, a baritone, Mummy, a tenor for the occasion, Harriet, the soprano and I, the alto, making a quartet in the car the rest of the journey home.

Mr Thomas, Daddy's boss, a rotund, kind, likeable man, was often at the restaurant and would spoil Harriet and me. We were always invited by him and his stately wife and mother for drinks on Christmas Day with strict orders from Mummy not to move from our seats. We waited longingly for the chocolates which were eventually offered and Mummy instructed us to take the chocolate nearest to us. Judith Bailey, Cornish Academy friend, composer and clarinettist, reminded me recently that she remembers us as a trio performing for them but that had escaped my memory. Parties for the firm's chosen members were held at Christmas time and crackers given contained miniature bottles of liquor. What fun when I took mine to school! All the children were suddenly very, very happy! Mummy used to be a little apprehensive when Mr Thomas dropped in at our bungalow to talk business with Daddy but when invited to supper he always stayed and enjoyed Mummy's cooking. I have a beautiful wedding cutlery set which he gave me when I married and I still use it every day.

My headmaster, Mr Benney, 2nd on the right with teachers and trustees at Four Lanes Primary School which I attended

At Four Lanes Primary School Mr Benney, the Headmaster asked if I would look after Penny, his granddaughter. We became great buddies

There came a time when Harriet and I had to take the 11+ to be considered for Helston Grammar School. Harriet, of course, passed with flying colours but I sadly failed it. This was due, I say, to Harriet being coached in the class by the headmaster, Mr Benney, while a year later Mr Flan arrived as headmaster and my class was not coached. That is my story but I didn't ever study much at all when I was young. I loved riding my bike around the village and beyond, stopping at the playing field where I developed my arm muscles by lifting myself over a bar time and time again for fun. I guess I didn't realise I had any good muscles until years later, when an artist friend, Jules George, said, "Where did you get those?" pointing at them on the beach at Milford-on-Sea, the nearest beach I now frequent from my home in Lymington.

I digress, but I did eventually go to grammar school because Mummy, who was a governor there, had contacts and used them. She argued that unless I went to a grammar school, I would not be given the musical training which she assessed was totally necessary for my future life.

"Could Wendy be given an interview so that you can make your own assessment?" she said. It seems unheard of but they agreed and eventually decided after my interview that if my work was not of the necessary standard in the first year then I could not continue. I was coached constantly by my teacher, Mummy, for the interview and for the following year at the Grammar School by Mummy every day in order to attain the standard required. I was, top of the class. Mummy was a brilliant teacher! My first day at the Grammar School I was without uniform as I only heard of my success the previous day. Before I leave this chapter, perhaps I should tell you a little of the romantic side of my life. At primary school I fell in love with a lovely little boy called Alan. He was gorgeous but knew nothing about how I felt.

CHAPTER TWO

At Helston Grammar School

❧

After my solo romance I was off to Helston Grammar School but not without interesting events. Harriet was already a pupil at the school. We travelled nine miles to school each day by bus, Harriet quietly sitting in the lower seating area and I on the top deck where there was much more fun with naughty boys. We did not arrive at school in time for the Assembly and had to leave early in the afternoons to catch the bus home. It was an interesting, hilly journey, passing the nine standing stones near Nine Maidens Primary School. The story goes that nine dancers daring to dance on a Sunday were turned into stone and the fiddler who had played for them was terrified by what he had done. These stones, so I understand, inspired the Cornish composer, George Lloyd, to write an opera about one of the dancers whom he envisaged as a fairy.

The journey to school was usually uneventful through Burras, Crelly, Trenear and Wendron to Helston until the winter snows came. On one occasion because of the unusually deep snow the bus was unable to get up the hill from Burras and we were just left there while the bus made its way back to Helston. We learned later that the school was not happy about this and thought that we should have been taken back to Helston and put up for the night.

Harriet and I still at Grammar School, shopping before joining our colleges in London

"One must learn from one's mistakes and never let it happen again." Haven't we heard that nowadays maybe too often! Nevertheless, we walked about two miles through a blizzard to Nine Maidens where the father of my friend, Valerie, picked us up with a suitable vehicle. There was no room for all of us but I was lucky and arrived home to find Nana, my granny, in tears, with Mummy and Harriet in a terrible state fearing we would be swallowed up in the blizzard. Two fresh saffron buns Mummy made had never tasted so good. Harriet sensibly hadn't been to school that day!

As Yum Yum in Helston Grammar School's production of Gilbert & Sullivan's The Mikado, *'Three Little Maids from School are we'.*

Doctor Weymouth and I arrived at the school during the same year, which was lucky for me as there wasn't a music teacher before him. It was advantageous also that at grammar school there was the headmaster's wife, Delphine Martelli, a professional solo pianist. I was immediately placed with her as my teacher and we sailed through the Associated Board of the Royal Schools of Music exams on the piano and with Dr Weymouth, the singing exams. The physics teacher, Mr Holden, rather rotund and not too jolly, asked me to be *Little Buttercup* to his *Captain* in Gilbert and Sullivan's *HMS Pinafore* in a concert. As I recollect Mummy said that if I was to rehearse in his home then I should take his elderly mother some chocolates. They were Maltesers. Mr Holden opened them, dropped them and then continued to eat most of them. He also would twist my ears when he decided that I wrote his comments too quickly in physics lessons. I had chosen Physics in case I went for Domestic Science as my future career as one of the subjects required was physics. Mr Dare, the English teacher, a keen tenor himself, together with Dr Weymouth, the music master, thought it a wonderful idea if they put on a stage performance of Gilbert and Sullivan's *The Mikado*. The cast would be Mr Dare as *NankiPoo*, me as *Yum-Yum* and of course Mr Holden as *Pooh-Ba* together with many other of the school's talented singers. We all had to provide our own costumes. I made a red kimono in silk for which, as I recall, the material was bought in Plymouth. This was a journey we took each year to get our new clothes for Harvest Festival, even though the car would always have punctures at least twice on the way up. Daddy usually found kind drivers who stopped to help him but one in doing so managed to steal his expensive trilby hat, an event never to be forgotten by the family. The Mikado performance was a great success and we all absolutely loved it. I also fondly remember a trio of speaking voices in which I was involved.

> *"Do you remember an Inn Miranda,*
> *Do you remember an Inn?"*

The idea of spoken voices only happened the once. I asked, "Why only on one occasion, why not *more* wonderful poetry?"

An amusing school episode was when Mr Skinner, the maths teacher, said, "Now tonight I want you all to do three more pages of algebra equations as it is Guy Fawkes' night and it is much safer to stay indoors."

Mummy said that it must be a joke but I was convinced it was not. Of course, I asked my sister, Harriet, to help out which she duly did and so I still enjoyed the evening. The next day Mr Skinner was greatly amused and took me into the staff room, sitting me on his lap while the teachers there had a great laugh at my expense. As a present though I did get some biscuits and thereafter was quite spoilt in maths classes and was even spared a few classes so that everyone could catch up. I dashed into the domestic science room where Miss Williams, the young teacher with whom I had a great rapport, let me join in her cooking session, which I loved. That day it was toad-in-the-hole which I took home. My Great-Auntie Lily, my grandmother's sister, kept a grocery shop next door to our bungalow and Mummy thought that we should share my food with her and Uncle Jim, which we did. Sadly, overnight Uncle Jim died of a heart attack – hopefully not because of my cooking though!

My mother was kind and supportive and helped me a lot as a teacher

The mock GCEs were approaching, and since I did not do at all well, I was summoned to see the headmaster, Mr Guise. Some parents and pupils were by this time aware that Mr Guise would cane the pupils' bottoms in the presence of the senior mistress, Mrs Smith. Mr Guise had, as I remember, a foot-long clothes brush to be used in punishment if he thought the work was not good enough. I was warned by Mummy beforehand that if this were to happen then I should literally, as she put it, "Go for him!"[1] The moment of truth came and I did tell him what my mother had said. I was very nervous making such a statement but he just said, "Don't pick your nose, Wendy," going on to say that he would be expecting much better results in the future.

I did get the results I was expecting in the exams, as I didn't study but focused my interest on the subjects that I really loved. I obtained English Language, with Mummy's keen guidance. Mr Skinner paid me great interest as the new, only girl in the maths top class and it annoyed the boys that I got a distinction. Music, of course, flowed so easily into my

---

[1] *The Cornishman*, Penzance July 9, 1964
Ex-Helston Headmaster and suspended Senior Mistress fined for beating girl pupils.

consciousness. Later I added Domestic Science and English Literature. Mummy read the books for me! I did think at one point that I might leave the school and get a job but to do what? One suggestion was that I might take some sort of job at the Royal Naval Air Station at Culdrose. I can only imagine that Mummy and Daddy had some sort of connection there. That idea soon faded and going back to school seemed the safest bet. The dilemma was what were to be my subjects in the Sixth Form. I loved cooking and sewing and hid in the tin cupboard when Dr Weymouth, the music master, came looking for me. In the second year I applied for Southlands College and went about producing samples of needlework for the interview, which went well. In the meantime, Delphine Martelli, my piano teacher, stressed to Mummy that I really should do music and was there any particular aspect in music that would interest me. My answer came that I wouldn't mind doing singing but had no idea what a vast subject it was and how technically skilled I needed to be. Maybe to be a music teacher and come back to Cornwall to teach was the safest idea. Dr Weymouth, also present at the meeting, was now in a position to suggest that in one year I could do advanced music and have the qualification to apply to a college of music. I readily agreed. Ernestine, a lovely kind friend, and I studied A Level together. I got a distinction which was helpful. Many years later we met at Trinity College of Music, where she was the librarian and I a teacher of singing and subsequently Head of Vocal Studies, Opera and Music Theatre. My only application was to the Royal Academy of Music, as Mummy considered that if I didn't get offered a place there then my chances were slim for any other college.

Daddy said, "Olga, if you send them to London, we will never see them again."

Auntie Clarice, a maiden aunt, popping into our bungalow after the evening service at the chapel, said, "And Harriet, what are you going to do now dear?" to which Harriet replied, "I am going to Bedford College in Regents Park, part of London University, Aunty Clarice."

"Lovely dear, and Wendy, what are you going to do?" to which I replied, "I am going hopefully to the Royal Academy of Music, Auntie Clarice."

"Oh!" says Auntie Clarice, "you have to be really clever to go there, dear," after which Daddy intervened, "She has these big ideas, Clarice, take no notice."

It didn't help having a clever studious sister, but I was so proud of her. A teacher at the grammar school scolded, "Wendy, if you had a quarter of the brain of your sister that would be good!"

Daddy said to me, "How do you expect to get on, Wendy, if you don't study?"

Is it really surprising when I had such a cavalier approach, didn't study and even in the domestic science room was looking out of the window to see if my supposed boyfriend, Keith, was going onto the playing field and if so I could go and talk to him?

The Latin teacher, Mrs Holden, wife of the science teacher, said to Mummy, "Did you know that Wendy goes into the playing field at school and meets a boyfriend?" and Mummy said, "Yes, I do know!"

Mummy didn't tell me what Mrs Holden's reaction was. However, I was dumped by Keith for his next liaison and felt heartbroken.

Mummy and I set off for the interview in London on the steam train from Redruth Railway Station, sandwiches, drinks and music all safely with us. Mummy had booked accommodation in Sussex Gardens, at a place where a number of Cornish people stayed when visiting London. All was going well until my throat felt rather sore. I mentioned to Mummy that I thought I was developing a cold. She was exasperated and said, "Wendy, this is typical of you. We are going all the way to London and now you think you have a cold!" as if I had arranged it on purpose.

However, feeling rather nervous during my interview at the Royal Academy of Music, I started singing Schumann's *Mondnacht*, a tenor Lied, the German language for which I had had special lessons with the German teacher at Helston Grammar School. The examiner, Sir Thomas Armstrong, the principal of the Royal Academy said, "Stop! You will ruin your voice with an infection like that. Can you do anything else?"

"Well, sir, I have just done my Grade VIII piano exam." I had no piano music with me but was able to play my three pieces from memory.

Dr Weymouth had advised that I take a small musical composition with me and so I also gave him that to view. When I found it recently it was quite pathetic and Michael and I had quite a laugh about it. Anyway, Mummy explained my predicament to Sir Thomas and a while later my result was received with a studentship to study piano as my major along with singing as secondary. Basically, the wonderful, kind and beautiful Delphine Martelli got me through.

I had no boyfriends, apart from minor liaisons with Alan, David and Eric, with whom I cycled in the village, flirting a little in Love Lane. Daddy decided to keep an eye on me and one time discovered my parked bicycle there. It wasn't good for me when I returned home! I had no serious attachments so went happily off to London in the steam train. Whenever we left the carriage window open, we were covered in soot and the smell was potent, but my future looked rosy.

CHAPTER THREE

The Royal Academy of Music

❄

M ummy drove Harriet and me to Redruth station where we waited for the steam train, which in those days was always late. Mummy saw us depart, crying and waving until we were out of sight. Her last words were, "Now you promise me that you will meet once a week!"

For the next three years we did lunch each week, on alternate Thursdays either at Harriet's college, Bedford College in Regent's Park, or what was almost around the corner, the Royal Academy of Music. I couldn't wait to leave lovely Cornwall and start a new adventure. It has been as good as I could have hoped for as I look back on my life now.

How does one find lodgings in London? Mummy and Daddy knew Mr and Mrs Bailey, who lived in Camborne and whose daughter, Judith, had also been accepted for the Academy as a clarinettist. On the steam train to London Judith introduced me to Jennifer Burrell, a pianist, both of whom had been pupils at Truro High School. Their Cornish accents were much less strong than mine. Did they rehearse, I wonder, "It makes you laugh to see a cow go down the path to have a bath." I think they did!

I guess much research went on, as eventually all three of us were ensconced in Miss Askew's house in Seymour Road, Finchley, after the long train journey. Our trunks would arrive on the day of travel or a day later. Quite a number of us stayed there, maybe sixteen girls in all, to study at the Royal Academy of Music. I shared a room with Jean Umpleby and Marjorie Dutton. Miss Askew, a formidable but kindly lady, looked after us well. There were to be no boyfriends in our rooms in the house but we could meet them in her lounge, though not after six o'clock in the evening. An imposing gentleman also appeared at times, mostly at weekends. I remember our introductory tea where we met many girls.

Miss Askew said to one, "And what would you like to drink?" to which she replied, "Do you have any pure lemon juice?"

I don't remember Miss Askew's reply but I was a little amazed and thought, Well this is London, I suppose.

I so remember my friendship with a Welsh student, Christine Gollop, a pianist at Askew Land, as we called it. One evening Christine said, "Let's go out in the smog and have a look!"

I wasn't too keen but we giggled our way along the road, seeing very little. At one point a gentleman got out of his car then came over to us and said, "Would you mind walking in front of the car to take us home? It's not too far."

"Let's do that, Wendy!" Christine said.

We did and he was so delighted that he gave us half a crown each, which I worked out would be roughly five pounds these days. At that time Harriet and I were given one pound each as our pocket money for the week. Naturally we didn't have to buy supper, which was provided at the lodgings throughout the year.

I had many wonderful times with Christine, who was, as I look back, a girl of the sixties, whilst I was a rather green girl from Cornwall. Some time later she contacted me to say that she was at King Edward VII Hospital in London. Naturally I went to see her and on arrival she said, "Now what would you like to drink, Wendy? I have sherry and red wine."

Sherry it was and we chatted but not about her illness. She was now married to Peter and lived in Scotland and was very ill. My last conversation with her was when Peter rang and told me that she was seriously unwell and having her feet massaged but wanted to speak to me. We had a short quiet chat. I made some trivial remark about her feet and Peter then took the phone and I imagine she was utterly drained and not able to continue. I talk of Christine because she was very special. I bought a piano from her, a Broadwood, which I used for many years.

The day after our arrival in Finchley from Cornwall we walked to the station to take the direct Northern Line to Warren Street, the nearest station to the Academy without changing tube trains. I was having trouble with my knees, as I had never walked so fast and so far in Cornwall. What a wimp I was! We trotted up the steps to this welcoming building, passing through double doors and facing an impressive staircase. My life was to be based here for the next six years. It was wonderful! Singing and piano were my major interests at the Academy. I think I was fortunate in that my teacher, May Blythe, taught in Room 20, which was one of the elegant rooms on the first floor, with an open fire which needed attention every now and then. Miss Blythe was so kind and with her mastermind efficiency, copious technical skill and use of complicated exercises developed my voice in strength and technical awareness over four years. She had in fact asked to teach me when she heard me at the audition for a scholarship.

At first, I graced Miss Blythe with a rendering of a Spohr aria.

> *Rose softly blooming, formed to allure,*
> *Emblem of nature, lovely and pure.*

"Wendy," she said, "we have to work on 'allure' and 'pure' and the 'r's'. Try this; 'Leoor' and 'Peoor.'"

I struggled! Lessons continued until one day she said, "I must mention, Wendy, that I don't think you have the voice for a singing career and so what were you hoping to do eventually?"

"Oh yes, I know that, Miss Blyth. I guess I will go back to Cornwall and teach." Whenever I developed a cold or throat infection Miss Blyth would say, "Wendy, go back to Cornwall. Get to the coast and breathe some good fresh air!" which I duly did! I am not sure it helped!

Listening to my friends in 1959, I realised that my standard was nowhere near as good as some of the singers who had had many professional lessons. In any case, Daddy had always said that I must get a teaching qualification so that I could make some money to live on if I was left at any time (by a husband I guess he meant). I continued loving my singing and piano lessons.

In my second year at the Royal Academy, I had promised my friend, Winifred Johns, at Helston Grammar that if she got into the Academy then I would find her a place in London to live with me. She was a super pianist and cellist. She joined me in Willesden Green in a private house where we ate heart and offal and other unusual dishes. No pasties! We survived and met another Academy student living with us. Winifred and I shared our snacks with her as she didn't seem to have any of her own until we were aware that she stored them under her bed.

We were told by the lady of the house that if we answered the door, we must not mention names of the visitors, particularly men! I did have a boyfriend there, Peter, a friend I met in Cornwall before I left for London. He visited me for a while until the trip from Eltham was too inconvenient and who can blame him. Winifred, Harriet and I met at Hynde Street Methodist Church every week on a Sunday, where Winifred muttered uneasily, "Wendy, do you have to sing so loudly?"

Miss Blyth's solid breath control technique, I guess; and somehow I couldn't sing softly at that time. Maybe I loved the chance to practise my singing. I worked a lot with Winifred, who was so patient when I asked if she would play the accompaniment over and over again. Each time I repeated it I felt I was gaining many more ideas to put into the interpretation of the song. At least my singing was admired at the church by Trevor, whom I dated for some time. He was a lay preacher, clever, loved music and went to London University. He came to Cornwall in the summer to work, in order to see me, visiting our bungalow, where Daddy thought him rather possessive.

Daddy's observation, "He even waits outside the bathroom door for you!"

Trevor eventually became a professor at Oxford University. I didn't marry him but I met my future husband, Geoffrey Pratley, a few years later at the Academy, the Marriage Bureau for so many of us! Naturally, at the Royal Academy of Music if we were to be performers and needed to represent this elegant institution then we had to know how to behave on the platform and how to present ourselves, including walking on and off the stage. Mrs Deller was our coach as we walked one by one towards her and passed her while she gave her judgement. On all accounts we should not cross our legs on the stage but always sit upright and dress appropriately. She attended many performances and was always there to address any issues she thought not applicable. My piano teacher, Russell Chester, was elegant in his tailored suit, sitting firmly beside me without a hint of a smile. I was really scared of him and worked solidly in the hope of pleasing him. I was for two years with him while my singing course progressed, but he wanted me to take serious exams in piano. By this time I was completely involved with singing and I explained this to him.

His reaction was, "Wendy, you are my best student!"

I was flattered, and thereafter not scared, however I knew that it was the right time to move if I was to take singing seriously. I was determined to be as good as my rivals, especially as a soprano, as there are always so many of us. I did however play for Winifred's cello exam and was approached by the examiner, Freddy Jackson, a piano professor, who offered to take me on as his student. A few years ago I mentioned this to Chris Elton, the Head of Piano at the Academy for many years, and he said, "What an opportunity and you turned it down!" Freddy was in fact the most respected piano teacher in the college. Sadly he later died while conducting a performance of the Verdi *Requiem*.

Onwards and upwards! I attended many lectures in the first and second years and spent time listening to Támás Vásáry, who was 26, a Hungarian concert pianist and conductor. This was in the Duke's Hall at the Academy, where he played the Bach Preludes and Fugues, which pleased me greatly.

The more exciting third year was approaching, when we could all be involved in the opera productions. Basically, this was an introductory course where all students from the singing teachers met to sing duets, trios, quartets in scenes from popular operas, coached by Mr Streets. He was calm but challenged us with very difficult music, for example, the trio from *Der Rosenkavalier* by Richard Strauss, with its slow high tessitura line in the role of *Sophie*. He polished languages, insisted on immaculate phrasing and balanced sound with male and female voices in the celebrated trio *Soave sia il vento* in Mozart's opera *Così fan Tutte*. We listened to our friends singing at last and discussed vocal technique in the canteen, describing at great length how our individual singing teachers taught us. I think we all benefitted a great deal from hearing various tips which we could use ourselves or at the very least use as an experiment. (The singers' table was the first on the left as we entered the canteen).

I loved all the male students I worked with at the Academy. The tall Richard Angus, later an English National Opera bass; Philip Langridge, a baritone who became a very distinguished international tenor; Paul Nemear, a baritone who also joined the West End show, *Robert and Elizabeth*; Barnaby Latham Sharp, a bass whose father was a composer; David Fisher, a tenor who was hilarious as a soldier in Mozart's opera *Così fan Tutte* and whose brother, Monti, became my accountant for many successive years. The male students did embarrass me at times, wanting to walk behind me going up the stairs to look at my ample bottom. I still meet some of the many students at parties. While at my home in Four Lanes, I arranged a supper party at Carn Brea Castle for Judith Bailey, whom I have already mentioned; Margaret Crosby, an Irish soprano and my wonderful friend who no longer lives near me and I so wish that I could see more often; Josephine Rippon, an Australian pianist and singer I met at the Academy, whose son 'Jonathan Rippon' is my very talented godson.

By the fourth year with non-stop practice my voice had changed remarkably into a deeper operatic sound. May Blyth's comment to me was, "Wendy, I have to say that you have made such amazing progress with your voice that I think after all you may be able to make a career as a singer!" I was delighted.

This led in February 1964 to my being offered firstly the role of *Fiordiligi* in Mozart's *Così fan Tutte*, the following years the role of *Angelica* in *Suor Angelica*, by Puccini and *Charlotte* in *Werther* by Massenet. These were in performances for the Opera Course productions, open to the public with national press reviews. We were able to choose our own dresses for the Mozart and I chose a deep purple for *Fiordiligi* which I thought contrasted with the rather flippant character of her sister, *Dorabella*. I didn't at all find it easy to portray the profound suffering of *Angelica* in the convent or the changeable moods of *Fiordiligi* in the Mozart, both very challenging roles. Vocally the singing roles were not problematic but releasing emotions was extremely difficult for me as I felt very self-conscious on the stage. It was very embarrassing and I felt guilty having been given the major roles. However, with much help I gained confidence and the press reviews were kind. It was not until later joining a West End show that repetition of performing every evening eventually solved the problem. But there were other changes that needed to be addressed. Even though I easily managed the runs in the difficult aria, *Come Scoglio* as *Fiordiligi*, they had to be produced differently to suit baroque composers such as Handel and Bach. With a heavy heart I had to talk to Miss Blyth about moving to another specialist baroque teacher to address the problem. Miss Blyth's reply was, "Well Wendy, I never used baroque runs and I made a very good living." Which of course she had done. She had been a celebrated operatic mezzo soprano and had worked in opera companies alongside her husband, the Australian conductor,

*Philip Language as Werther and I as
Charlotte in Massenet's Opera* Werther

Aylmer Buesst. She was extremely sad and somewhat hurt but knew that
as a soprano of small stature I had to tackle the problem for a possible
future career. Later after the Academy I did go back to her for some lessons
and always mentioned her in my CV as being the one person who
developed my child-like sound into a professional one over four years. I
shall never forget her incredible kindness.

"Wendy, have you seen the notice board?" said Faith one day.

"No," I said.

"Well, they have given you a scholarship for the next two years to
study!" Naturally I was delighted. This allowed me time to work on
baroque runs, which I used to do so easily before my voice was
operatically and technically developed but certainly didn't have then the
power in my voice that was developed with Miss Blyth. At the Academy
we could contact Myers Foggin, the Director of Opera, to discuss a new
teacher. Mummy suggested that Dame Eva Turner, a teacher at the
Academy, should teach me. Dame Eva was a huge celebrity, of course, but
Mr Foggin, keeping a watchful eye on my development, thought it was
time that I changed teachers. He suggested Flora Nielson, another mezzo
soprano, who was originally a soprano, to tackle the runs, and so I stayed
on for another two years. It was not a happy association, as she was rather
demeaning. Her main solution was placement, which took me some time

to understand. I plodded on with Geoffrey Pratley as my allocated pianist, who on one occasion witnessed me in tears over her steely remarks. She gave me the complete bound volumes of the Gilbert and Sullivan operettas with the comment, "I think that you, Wendy, are the only one of my students who will make use of them," referring to other singers being operatic stars, recitalists or a recording artist as she herself was primarily, so I'm told. It was a very kind gift and even though I didn't spend my career singing at all with the *Doyly Carte Gilbert and Sullivan Company* I did select solos from them for concerts and later my students were able to make use of them.

I saw her when I was leaving the Academy and am pleased to say that when Flora Nielsen asked me what I was doing I was able to tell her of my many accolades at English National Opera, Covent Garden and, of course, my many solo performances for the Henry Wood Promenade concerts held at the Royal Albert Hall each year.

It was while we were working together that Geoffrey Pratley mentioned that Astra Desmond, another eminent singing professor at the Academy, would like to teach me *Haugtussa*, a song cycle by Grieg, in the Norwegian *Landsmal* dialect and Sibelius songs in the Swedish language. Geoffrey Pratley would play for me and we would visit her home for the free tuition. This was an amazing opportunity which we relished, and we were extremely happy when the BBC asked us to broadcast the first performance in this country of the cycle. It was to be the start of my broadcasting career both in this country and abroad.

I have written about my two singing professors at the Academy but Geoffrey also advised me to have some tuition with specialist teachers on certain singing styles. llse Wolf, one of the great German Lieder singers of her generation; Gwen Catley, the English coloratura soprano known for her clarity and agility of voice, particularly in florid operatic arias; Bruce Boyce, a large tall man, a recitalist, oratorio and opera singer noted for flexibility, nuance of expression and sureness of touch in mood depiction and, not least, Dame Eva Turner, renowned for her clarion power in Italian and German operatic roles.

"Wendy, you have lost it!" she would say when referring to operatic long legato lines that lost tone just for a second! I feel privileged that I have studied with these wonderful artists and for the support of Geoffrey Pratley, who was at the time the pianist for recitals with Paul Tortelier,

Dame Janet Baker and Ralph Holmes. Believe it or not, it was only when I was singing in seven performances a week that I really understood how difficult it was to acquire a vocal technique that I really understood and that was good enough to tackle the most difficult repertoire.

Geoffrey Pratley, my pianist at college and later my husband

Geoffrey met the composer Michael Head in South Africa, both as examiners for the Associated Board of the Royal Schools of Music, and suggested that he might write a song cycle for me using Cornish Poets. His *Nine Cornish Songs* were later published in 2007 by Roberton Publications. I gave the first performance in the Duke's Hall at the Royal Academy of Music and then broadcast the first live performance for the BBC.

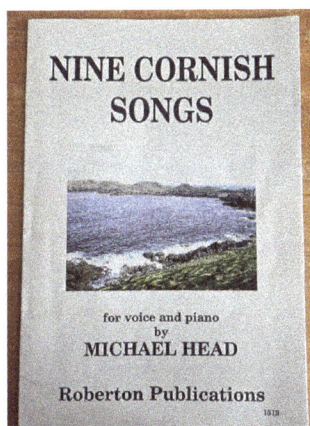

Nine Cornish Songs *by Michael Head*

At the Academy promising singers are offered paid engagements. One I remember well was when Philip Langridge and I were offered an engagement in Germany. On arriving the organiser said, "Well, do you speak German?" to which we replied, "Sadly, no," to which he replied, "Then you must be English!" This was not a particularly good start. Thinking of my future career I was naïve, maybe, but having pleased Daddy in getting a teaching qualification I had no financial worry for the future.

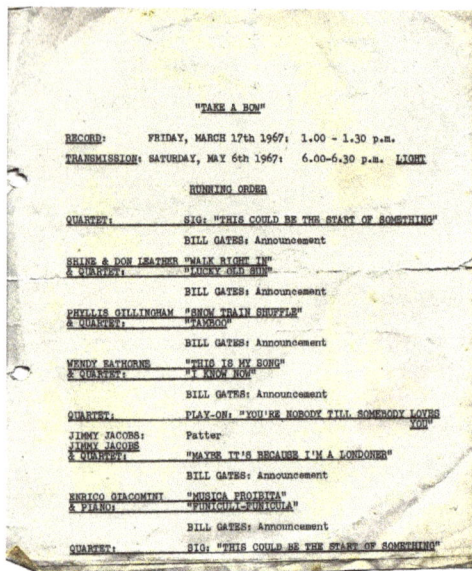

The Running Order for a BBC programme

It was only when I was looking at the singers' noticeboard, where auditions were offered for petite singers to join the petite June Bronhill in Ron Grainer's new production of *Robert and Elizabeth*, that I was persuaded by my friends at the Academy to go for it. Naturally having been trained as a classical singer this was not something that I really wished to do but I did go along. Wendy Toye, the producer, and the musical director, Andrew Farris offered me one of the two soprano places in the ensemble with a solo line *"For Ever and Aye"* all on one note. With my new agent, Margherita Stafford, I was reluctantly now stuck on the West End stage. However, there were advantages during my contract in the West End as there was time to record songs for Bill Gates' radio programme *"Take a Bow"* There was another programme for *Take a Bow*. I sang *This is my Song* and guess what! *I Know Now* from *Robert and Elizabeth*.

CHAPTER FOUR

Robert and Elizabeth

❦

O n October 20th 1964 I appeared on the West End stage at the Lyric Theatre in Shaftesbury Avenue in the musical, *Robert and Elizabeth*, based on the story *The Barretts of Wimpole Street* by Rudolph Besier. Little did I realise that this was to be one of the most rewarding and essential parts of my singing career. Being on stage for eight performances a week certainly got rid of any stage inhibitions and also, with the help of Wendy Toye giving me a solo stage entrance as an old crippled waitress it ensured I would easily portray believable characterisations during my future career. It ran for 948 performances and was previewed in Manchester, where I stayed in digs on the Oxford Road and for many evening suppers had the landlady's macaroni cheese which was in fact quite delicious.

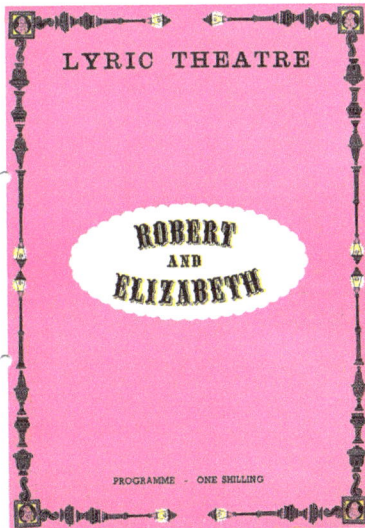

The programme of Robert & Elizabeth, *the show I was in for two years*

Keith Michell drew this picture of me in the interval of the show

In London at the Lyric Theatre I shared the dressing room on the top floor with one soprano, two mezzo soprano singers and four lady dancers. We mingled together happily and at each performance raced up and down the stairs (700 steps) for our stage entries. Jennifer Conway, who was to marry Ron Grainer, the composer, managed to persuade Keith Michell, Robert Browning in the show, to do a portrait of all the ensemble girls. I still have mine hanging on the wall at the top of the stairs in my Hampshire home.

Looking out of the window in our dressing room overlooking Windmill Street it was a complete eye-opener when Anita said to me, "Oh, look Wendy, there's a pimp!"

"Wendy, we are going to a ball'." I had other visions!

The time between the matinée and the evening performances twice a week gave us all ample opportunity to shop and what better place than Soho's market? I was able to take home wonderful vegetables and particularly liked the material shop, where I had a choice of textiles and fabrics from many parts of the world. Not only that, but from a deli I devoured salt beef sandwiches unlike any I have ever tasted. One day on my way back from shopping I noticed a crowd of people engulfing what seemed to be a celebrity of note. It did not take me long to realise that it was around the great Mohammed Ali, who was extolling his greatness and of course I think he was the greatest!

Going to the party of the leading lady, June Bronhill, and seeing a bath full of ice and champagne was sparklingly good. I guess I was invited because at the time I was June's seamstress and did some alterations to her beautiful costumes. Of course, we were all chosen in the ensemble to match the leading lady's petite stature. There was great excitement in the dressing room one day when I announced that I was getting married to Geoffrey Pratley whom I had met at the Royal Academy of Music. We all discussed the wedding preparations and I was given two free days off for the wedding and honeymoon. I was allowed no more as they were very strict on absenteeism.

The wedding day photo at the reception in the Falmouth Hotel in Cornwall

Off to Cornwall, where we were married in the village church, St Andrews, in Four Lanes, the village where I was born. Later a fabulous reception at the Falmouth Hotel where I was persuaded to sing and chose a solo from *Robert and Elizabeth*:

> "I know now why all the world is fine and fair
>   And why there's music in the air to listen to.
> If all the world is fine and fair
>   And if there's music in the air, the song is you."

We stopped off at Exeter on the way back to London for the brief honeymoon then straight off to the Lyric Theatre the next day. There was a small reception for me at the Theatre when I was presented with a fridge, which was useful and a very kind present. Keith Michell presented me with it and after a pause when he tried to think of my name said the usual kind comments. My time in *Robert and Elizabeth* was uneventful. I took a train from our home in Bethnal Green to Piccadilly Circus every day except Sunday. During the daytime I continued my lessons at the Academy but singing for eight performances a week and practising each day difficult challenging arias for future auditions had an adverse effect on my voice. My good legato line had vanished and it certainly needed to be addressed. I chose a German Lied to work on my voice. I thought that if I looked in the mirror, checked any tension in my face, relaxed my breathing, felt the circular motion and worked from note to note using vocal technique all acquired from my teachers, my voice could only improve. Thankfully it did, but I realised that professional singing is only comfortable and possible if one totally understands and is confident and capable of an advanced and secure technique, particularly for opera.

One evening there was an eventful performance at the theatre. Keith Michell had a song using a trumpet and was warned by Wendy Toye, the producer, to be careful when waving the instrument about on stage as it could be dangerous. It was indeed dangerous! In one evening performance I was knocked out on the stage by one of his dramatic gestures. Quickly I was carried off and my husband, Geoffrey Pratley, was contacted to pick me up by the statue of Eros on Piccadilly Circus to take me home. I hastily left the theatre without bothering to remove my stage makeup.

As I stood on the pavement waiting for Geoffrey a policeman approached and said, "Move on please!"

I replied, "I have just been knocked out on the stage and I'm waiting here for my husband, who is picking me up."

He then said, "Well, I've heard a lot of stories but never that one before. Now please move along!"

It was a big mistake not to have removed my makeup. Obviously the policeman thought I was a *lady of the town*!

At The Lyric Theatre we had many audience admirers and on one occasion I received a bottle of Chanel perfume, but it came too late as I had just married my attentive, handsome and talented husband.

My contract was for two years plus the three-month review in Manchester and, even though I realised I was extremely lucky to be working in the West End with such famous people as Keith Michell, Sir Donald Wolfit, who took over from Sir John Clements, and June Bronhill, the Australian soprano, I was anxious for a challenge. This was to be when Margherita Stafford, a London agent, arranged an audition for me at Glyndebourne Festival Opera.

The cast and company of "Robert And Elizabeth" assembled on the stage of London's Lyric Theatre to present a refrigerator to 25-year-old singer Wendy Eathorne, who is appearing in her first West End musical and who is getting married on April 3. She comes from Four Lanes (near Redruth) and the ceremony will take place there. Her fiancé is Geoffrey Pratley, also 25, an accompanist from Woodford, Essex. The picture shows leading lady June Bronhill (right) presenting the gift to Wendy. Centre is Keith Mitchell, who plays Robert.

Receiving my present from the cast of Robert and Elizabeth *for my wedding to Geoffrey Pratley*

CHAPTER FIVE

Glyndebourne Festival Opera

❋

I couldn't have wished for more when, after a successful audition, I was immediately offered a position in the Glyndebourne Festival Chorus, whose quality and commitment makes it one of the pre-eminent choruses in international opera. This chorus at the time was run by Jani Strasser, the Head of Music. He was a formidable character with exceptional insight into voices and was only interested if applicants were promising soloists. During my time there I worked with Jill Gomez, Josephine Barstow, Theresa Cahill, Thomas Allen and Richard Van Allen, the names I particularly remember. My problem was how to get to Glyndebourne from London. The first year I decided to drive. I had to allow three hours to be sure of arriving on time for rehearsals but being invited to sing for the next three years I decided it was best and more sensible to stay in the vicinity of Glyndebourne.

As 1st Boy in Mozart's The Magic Flute *at Glyndebourne Festival Opera*

The whole ambience at Glyndebourne is startlingly impressive. Every aspect has been given the utmost attention. The grounds are glorious in the countryside, the workshops full of action, the restaurants enticing and the public in full evening dress, with picnic baskets and champagne all ready for a magical experience. Whilst performances were on, we as artists were only allowed in the grounds during the intervals if we too were in evening dress. Elegance was not to be compromised.

I was at Glyndebourne from 1967 to 1973, three years as a chorister and three as a soloist. I simply loved my time there. I found the opportunities that Glyndebourne offered me in those years both as a chorister and soloist shaped my career and the interests that I have now in my adult life. This is not forgetting my love of champagne developed by the taste of Moët & Chandon provided by Sir George Christie, the British Opera administrator and son of John Christie, founder of the world's renowned Opera House. He was delightful and charismatic. A charming, thoughtful and caring gentleman, so respected by everyone.

The first chorus opera in which I performed was Mozart's *Don Giovanni* directed by Peter Hall, who was married at that time to the French actress Leslie Caron and was later to become most influential in the theatre world. We appeared at a Promenade Concert of *Don Giovanni* at the Royal Albert Hall and a critic commented on the wonderful display of attire worn by the choristers and in particular one lady who wore a blue feather bowered dress and blue knickers to match!

In that same year in 1967 a tour of the Scandinavian countries was imminent and some of the chorus members were to be chosen. I waited tentatively to see whether or not I would be included. As luck would have it, I was.

We arrived in Stockholm by bus on the 3rd of September, the day on which the traffic in Sweden switched from driving on the left-hand side of the road to the right. It was a frightening but exciting experience with a few near mishaps. We performed at the Drottningholm *Slottsteater* in Stockholm and in Oslo for Den Norske Opera, during which time I was able to visit my Cornish home-village friend, Jennifer Jenkins, who had married a Norwegian she had met at Exeter University. We also performed at the *Stora Teatern* in Gothenburg and the *Falkoner Centret* in Copenhagen. My memories of Copenhagen are seeing the eels being skinned at the harbour and our visit to the Carlsberg brewery. There we

were invited to a tasting session when some of the male artists took full
advantage of the occasion.

Eugene Onegin by Tchaikovsky is best known for Tatianna's letter
scene where she declares her love for Onegin and where Lenski
challenges Onegin to a duel over Tatiana's sister, Olga. However, for me
the ball scene is just wonderful and I really wanted to join the girls to
dance. I did request it but sadly the girls were chosen for their height. The
choreographer did give me a little solo *mazurka* at the side of the stage
which pleased me no end. The other delightful moment in *L'Elisir
d'amore* by Donizetti is the girls' chorus which is so characterful when
they enjoy the secret that Nemorino the village boy has been left a legacy
by his uncle.

My progression moving as a member of the elite chorus for three years
to a soloist was when I was offered the role of First Boy in Mozart's *The
Magic Flute*. There were three Boys in all and we rode through the wings
on three large stage horses. Unfortunately, the Third Boy, mezzo soprano
Valerie Baulard, could only just get through the wings, which caused us
some merriment if suffering for Valerie. The second Boy, taken by the
soprano, Sylvia Eaves, I had already met on the West End stage in *Robert
and Elizabeth*. It was a very happy reunion. A much less happy occasion
was when Annon Lee Silver, the Canadian lyric soprano, passed away.
She had premiered the solo soprano part in Nicholas Maw's *Rising of the
Moon* and was a delightful Sophie in Massenet's Werther. It was such a
shock for everyone. As the understudy working on the roles, I was asked
to replace her. Having sung the role of Charlotte in the *Werther*
production at the Royal Academy of Music I was very familiar with the
role of Sophie, Charlotte's sister. I had to now become that lighter
supportive sister rather than the emotional and confused character of
Charlotte. The role of Atalanta in the Nicholas Maw was a different
challenge, with a high tessitura and a moment when Atalanta, a young
flippant character, sings *"What's an orgy?"* It was a special moment to
meet the Queen Mother when she came to a performance of the Maw
and it was obvious that she was completely familiar with the Thirty-First
Royal Lancers and so interested in their military attire. Apparently, she
loved the opera.

As Sophie in the opera Werther *by Massenet at Glyndebourne*

There was a moment at Glyndebourne when we were offered some David Hockney prints. Sadly, I did not buy one, which I regret as I am such an admirer of his paintings. As a soloist it was a special occasion for me when I was able to rehearse with a coach in the wonderful organ room, surrounded by grandeur at its best! The Italian coach at Glyndebourne, Ubaldo Gardini, once spent a whole hour with me on just one phrase until he was satisfied. It certainly was extremely useful when later in my career I was asked to sing the *Wesendonck Lieder* in Italian in Italy. They are five songs of significance because of their connection with Wagner's opera *Tristan und Isolde* where two songs are reworked in Acts II and III. As a soloist at Glyndebourne, I had many complimentary tickets for family and friends. On one occasion Dr Kingsley, my doctor, was the recipient of two tickets. He was overjoyed and so kind to me and later I was asked to speak at his funeral.

The Glyndebourne festival runs from May to August with rehearsals starting a month before, which means I had ample time during the rest of the year to pursue other invitations to sing. As well as Glyndebourne giving excellent tuition and opportunities to perform there it also acts as a shop window for employers.

In a smart day dress for trips overseas for competitions

This was the case with Raymond Leppard, who at the time was conducting Monteverdi's operas. He engaged me for a series of radio broadcasts, which we rehearsed in 1969 and recorded in 1970. I remember being extremely tense singing for him and came away with very sore cheeks. If he became frustrated, he would spell out the words of instructions. On one occasion I needed to be released so that I could take a train to Wales for a concert. Luckily my Cornish friend, the eminent baritone Benjamin Luxon, came to the rescue and I just caught the train in time. Later I did work with him again when he conducted *The Rising of the Moon* on the Glyndebourne tour. Being engaged by Glyndebourne for only the summer months of the year gave me a great opportunity to perform at other venues, but my husband, Geoffrey, thought I should enter prestigious competitions on the continent. My first was in 1968 for the *International Vocalisten Concours* in 's-Hertogenbosch, Holland where I was the second prize winner. This resulted in an immediate offer to perform as soloist in Verdi's *Requiem* and in Haydn's *The Seasons* at the Concertgebouw, Amsterdam under the baton of the eminent conductor, Haitink. This needed financial help and it was Geoffrey's idea to approach the philanthropist, Sir Robert Mayer, because he was at the time supporting music and young musicians. At first he refused, but when I won the second prize he immediately changed his mind and financed me. I remember attending his hundredth birthday at the Royal Festival Hall in a gala concert attended by the Queen. He died at the grand old age of 105.

In 1969 I was asked to represent England in the International Music Festival in Parsissicians organised by Unesco. Sadly, I was not successful but braved it to ask the eminent musician, Sir Yehudi Menuhin, for feedback. He was extremely helpful and said that I should have concentrated on a particular *Fach*. There were too many differing styles such as Opera, German Lied, French Song and so on but I should have used only one. According to my accompanist he said that the audition panel thought my dress was too revealing. It had a keyhole neckline!

My next attempt was for the most sought after *Calouste Gulbenkian Foundation Award*. This had a huge financial reward. I remember I could not stay to hear the other soloists nor could I stay for the announcement of the winner. I guess I had another singing engagement that day. Later I had a phone call from my friend, Sally Le Sage, to say that I was the winner of the competition. At first, I didn't believe her, but it was confirmed soon after. At the time the award was worth more than the house we had just bought. You could be wondering if I entered the Kathleen Ferrier Award, which I did. My feedback from the great Dame Eva Turner was that the panel thought Margaret Neville and I were very capable already to be professional soloists but the baritone needed the prize more than we did. Margaret Neville, who was also a student at the Academy at the time I was there, had a wonderful career in Germany.

While touring in England with the Welsh National Opera's "Opera for All" in 1968 came another opportunity to sing major roles: Karolina in Smetana's *The Two Widows* and Adina in Donizetti's *L'Elisir d'Amore*. Plenty to get on with in the characterisations of Adina, the country girl, the doctor and the lawyer. Karolina in the Smetana enjoys her new found freedom while her sister Anezka wears her widow's mourning in earnest.

Later I accepted at short notice the role of Adina again for the Welsh National Opera Company in Cardiff. I performed the staged production in just a week, with a good coach of course.

Basilica Opera was a smaller opera company in the sixties where I was fortunate enough to be offered the huge role of Margherita in Gounod's *Faust*. What a sing! A challenge, especially nearing the end of the opera, where the soprano repeats a sustained vocal line over and over again but each a semitone higher. I did thoroughly enjoy her prayer in the Church, with its gorgeous melody but not forgetting the *Jewel Song* and an array of numerous jewels to display. There I worked with a mezzo soprano friend, Pat Conti, whom I met at Glyndebourne, who later appeared in the West End show *The Sound of Music* as the Mother Abbess, taking over from the great Constance Shacklock.

CHAPTER SIX

The Whirlwind
Seventies and Eighties

❀

When I look back at the '70s and '80s it almost seems like a dream. It basically all started when, whilst at Glyndebourne, I was offered a contract with the English National Opera in 1970. There I sang Zerlina in *Don Giovanni*, Oscar in *The Masked Ball*, Frascita in *Carmen*, the Princess in *The Love for Three Oranges*, Papagena in *The Magic Flute* but most important of all, Cupid in *Semele*. It was there that the leading concert agents in London, Ibbs and Tillett, after hearing me engaged me as their artist. Before being inundated with engagements from them I was able to accept an invitation to sing at Covent Garden as the Esquire in Wagner's *Parsifal*. I was chosen for my petite stature, in contrast to the statuesque Martti Talvela as Gurnemanz. There were eight performances, scheduled to be conducted by Jascha Horenstein, but sadly he died before they were completed. What was so impressive at Covent Garden was the size of the stage. Enormous! Later I was unable to accept the role of Frascita in *Carmen* for Covent Garden as Ibbs and Tillett had already booked me for many oratorio and concert engagements both in this country and abroad. On one occasion I sang every night for twelve nights and on two occasions every night for nine nights. They informed me that I was very much in demand and the busiest soprano in the country. I was happily with the agent from 1975 to 1990.

Before my connection with the agent, I had a very long association with the Handel specialist, Charles Farncombe, from the 1970s until 1985. He was the founder and conductor of the Handel Opera Society. In 1972, five years after my visit to Sweden with Glyndebourne, Charles invited me back to Sweden on two occasions, one in a concert

*Playing the role of
Teofane in Handel's opera
Ottone with the Handel
Opera Society at Sadlers
Wells Theatre*

performance of Handel's *Solomon* at Göteborg and two years later
the part of Teofane in *Ottone*. This was in the 1762 Drottningholms
Slottsteater where Charles was the chief conductor. This time we were
warned that since the theatre was mostly constructed of wood, there was
the potential danger of fire. I learnt a great deal from Charles Farncombe.
A Handelian specialist, his knowledge of the art of recitative (when
telling the story between arias) was of enormous help. So often I put his
superlative ideas into practice in major roles at the Queen Elizabeth Hall
in London in so many of Handel's oratorios and operas. *Hercules, Alcina,
Alexander's feast, L'Allegro, Il Penseroso, Il Moderato* and *Susanna*; and
on the stage at the Sadlers Wells Theatre in *Jephthah, Giustino, Rinaldo*
and *Ottone*.

In 1978 Charles Farncombe invited me to sing the part of Cesto, in
Giulio Cesare at the theatre in La Besnardière in France, in collaboration
with the New Philharmonic Orchestra of Radio, France. Beautiful
costumes were hired from the Royal Opera House in Stockholm, I
worked with one of my favourite harpsichordists, Robert Aldwinkle, and
all the cast were treated to sumptuous meals by the locals twice a day.
These did little for our waistlines but were worth every moment.

As Sextus in Handel's
Julius Caesar *at La*
Besnardière in France

In October 1972 a broadcast recording of *The Pilgrim's Progress* by Vaughan Williams was a different matter. It was a daunting experience when I performed the part of the Woodcutter's boy with the conductor Sir Adrian Boult. He had a big beat with an extra-long baton and the freedom he gave frightened me. I did speak to a kind-looking eminent lady and said I was rather in awe of him and somewhat scared.

She said, "He always likes to give his singers space to be able to easily manage their own interpretations."

The lady was Lady Boult!

However, fun times were on the many occasions going to Ireland, always enjoying their humour and generous hospitality. The one disadvantage of going to Ireland was of course being in the on-going "troubles". Artists of Ibbs and Tillett were booked in at the Europa hotel in Belfast, which was bombed eventually no fewer than thirty-six times. I decided on one occasion not to stay at the Europa Hotel and ensconced myself in nearby lodgings, which proved to be not at all suitable. However, I trotted back to the Europa and thought it would probably be okay. They were checking the cases and bags when people arrived, so it seemed. They took one look at me and said, "Go ahead. We don't need to look in your case." So the problem in fact was still there, but I survived it. In fairness to my agent there were no other convenient hotels near the Ulster Hall. With the Ulster Orchestra and the Belfast Philharmonic Society I enjoyed singing in the *Messiah* and Beethoven's *Mass in C* with the conductors Alan Francis and Bryden Thompson respectively. I must not forget to mention my two engagements of Dvořák's *Requiem* at the City Hall and the Gaiety Theatre in Dublin, with the RTE Symphony Orchestra.

I first met Sir Charles Groves in 1973 in a performance of Mahler's *Eighth Symphony* at Alexandra Palace in London, before it was burnt down in July 1980. Twelve years later it was such a pleasure to work with him again in Ireland at the Ulster Hall, in one of my favourite pieces, Beethoven's *Missa Solemnis*. I later replaced Heather Harper, who was ill on the day, in a performance of this piece with the conductor Antal Dorati. It seems that Helen Watts didn't perform either, as I remember, that Alfreda Hodgson sang the contralto role, the Welshman, Stuart Burrows was the tenor and Gwynne Howell, the bass. I was already familiar with the latter as one of the conspirators in Verdi's *The Masked Ball* in which I played the role of Oscar for the English National Opera.

The Celtic atmosphere I experienced in Ireland was much the same in Cornwall and being Cornish I was totally spoiled by Mr Sinfield, or Sin as we used to call him, who engineered that on every possible occasion I was invited to Truro Cathedral to sing. He was aware that a good audience was very likely. It certainly didn't hinder my situation that Henry Mills, the County Music adviser, had known me at Helston Grammar School and agreed to finance me to the Royal Academy of Music as a student, helping and encouraging me every inch of the way. I am so grateful for all the support I have been given, especially in Cornwall. Sir David Wilcox, a Cornish gentleman from Newquay, engaged me on numerous occasions. A comment from my solicitor friend was, "Have you ever known anyone from Newquay being a Cornishman?" We met in 1971 when I performed Bach's *Magnificat* and Mendelssohn's *Hymn of Praise* at The Royal Festival Hall with the English Chamber Orchestra in the Ernest Read Concerts for Children. As musical director and conductor of the Bach Choir, Sir David engaged me in many more performances at the Royal Festival Hall and to my delight chose on one occasion Tippett's oratorio, *A Child of our Time*, giving me the soaring soprano line in one of the Five Negro Spirituals. I certainly was lucky to be offered performances of my favourite compositions. Another with Sir David was Mahler's *Symphony No.8* (The Symphony of a Thousand), performed at the Royal College of Music where Sir David was the principal. This Symphony has three major soprano roles and I have sung all three of them in three different performances: second soprano with Sir David Wilcox, third soprano with Sir Charles Groves in Alexandra Palace and first soprano for the Henry Wood promenade concert, with the conductor Pierre Boulez.

Sir David chose Handel's *Israel in Egypt* as the piece to be performed in three different venues on a West Country Tour: Wells Cathedral, Exeter Cathedral and Truro Cathedral. We all travelled by bus to accommodate these three different venues and on the way to Truro Cathedral Sir David suggested that we might join him for a swim. Some adventurous choir members joined him on what I remember was not the most pleasant day but I was invited by the tenor, William Kendall, to join him crabbing. Not successful of course but a fun time!

As Papagena with John Gibbs as Papageno in The Magic Flute *at the English National Opera*

It is an unusual experience to be able to have a rehearsal with the conductor other than on the day of the performance and this was mostly the case with Roger Norrington, especially abroad. In Leuven in 1972 for Belgium Radio and Television I was invited by Roger Norrington to sing with the Heinrich Schütz Choir in recording the music of late Renaissance and early Baroque. Being televised, my short stature was a slight problem for the occasion and so I provided a little stool to give me some height. My first encounter with the conductor had been in Cornwall. On the way to Prussia Cove for a performance there was a problem with a rehearsal venue, so I offered my parents' home in Four Lanes as the rehearsal venue for a concert that evening. Mummy wished to know from me when she could provide us with a drink if needed. It worked well! It is interesting now to know that Prussia Cove is renowned for the annual International Musicians' Seminar given there.

Haydn's *Creation* is a massive sing for the soprano soloist and Roger Norrington was keen to work with me on the two arias in particular, *With Verdure Clad* and *On Mighty Pens*. We rehearsed in the organ loft at Westminster Cathedral, with Roger giving me his interpretations of the arias. I was totally inspired by him and added his ideas in performances whenever I performed the work again. The occasion was a performance at Westminster Cathedral for the International Festival of Flowers and Music. It was a good month, July 1977.

My introduction to Belgium by Roger Norrington meant that my agent had many more invitations for me to sing in the major cities. On one occasion after a concert, we as soloists were the only ones booked to travel on a flight back to Gatwick. The officials, knowing that there was a private flight going to Gatwick, cancelled the scheduled flight. Our tickets were taken from us and we were escorted onto a little plane where they had to use jump leads to start the engine. It was a frightening journey but at least we got back to England for our commitments the next day.

When giving my life history hardly a moment goes by without my mentioning Cornwall in some way or other. Soon after being at the Royal Academy, I was invited by Richard Hickox to perform in Cornwall at the beautiful St Endellion Church, beloved by Sir John Betjeman. It is one of England's holy places, an ancient Collegiate church with six prebends.

The role of Cupid in Handel's Semele *at the English National Opera at the Coliseum*

The English composer Michael Tippett wrote a song cycle, *The Heart's Assurance*, with five songs which are the most remarkable and fearless settings of poetry by young men who fought and died in the Second World War. Since I had studied these settings with Geoffrey, my future husband, during my time at the Royal Academy, I was delighted to be asked to perform them at St Endellion Church. In complete contrast to those emotional settings, I performed the major roles in two major operas at the church, *Idomeneo* and *la Clemenza di Tito* with Richard Hickox again as conductor. The vicar was a little apprehensive about performing operas in the church and decided that there should be no clapping. The enthusiastic audience, however, could not be restrained and won the day! I travelled from my home in Four Lanes to the Church, much to Mummy's delight at seeing me. After one concert on a trip home late at night, I was concerned to notice the petrol gauge was showing empty. To my relief, I soon came to a filling station. But my relief was short-lived. The garage was closed. I took a chance and knocked on the door of the house next door to the petrol station. By a stroke of luck, it happened to be the garage owner's, so all ended well.

Back to London and St Margaret's, Westminster, where Richard was organist. I was frequently invited to sing with the Richard Hickox Orchestra and St Margaret's Westminster Singers. A memorable occasion of mine was the Monteverdi *Vespers*, a concert for deprived and handicapped children. Another was Bach's *Mass in B Minor* where I joined the tenor in a duet and the alto in two duets, all three wonderfully satisfying to perform. Due to Richard Hickox's connection with Cornwall and love of the place he asked me to work with him as soloist in two performances of Beethoven's *Missa Solemnis* at Truro Cathedral and at Wells Cathedral. I later made gramophone recordings with him as soloist in Bach's four *Short Masses* and Schubert's *Mass in A*.

Even after singing at Glyndebourne, appearing at English National Opera and Covent Garden and with much experience on the concert platform, it was a great joy to be given the opportunity to sing the *Four Last Songs* of Richard Strauss and to broadcast them in April 1973 in an orchestral concert with the BBC Northern Symphony Orchestra, conductor Stewart Kershaw. It was a piece I had always longed to perform with the soaring soprano lines and the wonderful violin solo played by

On the left as the Esquire in Wagner's Opera, Parsifal *at the Royal Opera House, Covent Garden*

the leader in the song *September*, the second song in the cycle. After six months it was a bonus to perform the piece again with The Royal Philharmonic Orchestra under David Atherton for the Hemel Hempstead Festival.

It was after ten years, in May 1984, when I dressed with my hair scraped back like a ballet dancer that I tried to emulate the dancers of the London Festival Ballet when I was engaged to accompany them as they danced to my performance of the Strauss *Four Last Songs* yet again. I performed them in the pit at the London Coliseum and appeared briefly for a bow on the stage. It was quite a different conception to interpret the songs as I was very conscious of the rhythmic structure and controlled tempo so essential for the dancers.

Let us turn to the composer, Johann Sebastian Bach. At the time Paul Steinitz, the founder and conductor of the London Bach Society, was aiming to complete his BBC recordings of all the Bach Cantatas luckily, he succeeded in doing this before he died. What is more, he always used period instruments. They have such an unforgettable impact on any audience who are then able to experience a true authentic style.

Looking through my radio and concert programmes I see that I performed many times for Dr Steinitz at the Queen Elizabeth Hall in radio performances and a promenade concert at the Royal Albert Hall. I wondered at the time if he would invite me to sing *Cantata 210*, which is one of the most difficult. How did Bach compose forty-five minutes of coloratura singing in this cantata? It expresses the joyous and exuberant emotion of one's wedding day with its ravishingly beautiful tunes. I did perform the *Cantata 210* at the Queen Elizabeth Hall but not *Cantata 52*, another soprano masterpiece.

I have also had a long association with Dame Janet Baker. First and foremost, my husband, Geoffrey, was her pianist for many years and I would accompany them with her husband, Keith, who drove us to many venues. On one occasion Alice my daughter came with us as a baby but was too young to attend the concert. Janet asked me if she could hold Alice for a while in the car and of course I agreed, but only for a short while as Alice was a young baby with nappies and that was not a risk I wanted to take. Geoffrey was convinced that the reason Alice is so musical was due to her attending many of Janet's concerts. Particularly when I was pregnant Alice would kick me every time Janet sang. She was fascinated when I mentioned this to Janet recently.

My first performance as a soloist with Janet was on March 31st 1973 with Dr Steinitz at St Martin-in-the-Fields and ten years later again in Bach's *St Matthew Passion*. Perhaps the most exciting aspect of performances with Janet were the recitatives we enjoyed battling with in a BBC recording of Gluck's *Armide* in 1984, four years before Dr Steinitz died.

Dr Steinitz invited me on a tour of Germany in performances of Bach's *B Minor Mass*, visiting Potsdam and Berlin. These were both sides of the Berlin Wall including the Thomaskirche in Leipzig, where Bach had been the Kapellmeister. What an extraordinary experience! Bach's *Coffee Cantata* is one of his secular cantatas of which there are 50 out of approximately 300 cantatas. The *Coffee Cantata* could be described as a mini *buffo* opera.

The text highlights

> *"The desire to drink coffee is better than a thousand kisses or smoother than muscatel wine."*

I'm not so sure! The opportunity to perform this cantata came with Charles de Wolff, the conductor of the Netherlands Bach Society, in three performances in December 1976 at Stadskanaal, Groningen and Emmen in the Netherlands. It was a refreshing change to have drama in Bach that could be performed quite operatically. I was later invited by the same conductor to Naarden as the soprano in the *St Matthew Passion* and in the *B minor Mass* in Amsterdam, naturally with different interpretations of the religious texts.

I have lost count of the many performances of *Messiah* I have done in this country and abroad. I will mention my performance of this oratorio with the conductor, Henrik Rycken, in Etterbeek in Belgium in 1973. Mostly orchestras are able to accommodate my very fast speed which is my preference for Rejoice Greatly in *Messiah* and on this occasion we rejoiced exuberantly.

Apparently, the key of B♭ in which the aria was written is not an easy one for an orchestra technically. The London Philharmonic Orchestra are the tops in this respect. On occasions conductors have chosen a slower speed which does not give me the opportunity to express joyfulness nearly as much. Later in 1978 I worked with the same conductor, Henrick Rycken, at the Casino Beringen in Carl Orff's *Carmina Burana*, not a piece for the faint-hearted. The soprano sits for about thirty minutes before her entrance when there is a perilous moment on a top B natural followed by a soaring phrase including a D. This is not something I cherish as I am not a coloratura soprano.

How relaxing earlier that year to sing in a performance of Dvořák's *Stabat Mater* at the beautiful Palais de Beaux Arts, home of the National Orchestra of Brussels. There is a wonderful quartet "Quis est Homo" and a duet with the tenor "Fac ut portem Christi mortem". Not a soprano solo in sight! It sounds ridiculous after the wonderful musical opportunities I was given in Belgium but in consolation I did enjoy coffee in the Grande Place, the stylish central square in the city of Brussels, known for its decorative architecture and wealth. Perhaps I should mention that travelling abroad is not necessarily helpful to good singing, particularly when travelling by plane, as I suffered on many occasions from infections of the voice. If the infection was mild then I could manage my voice technically but on one occasion in Italy the voice was beyond repair and another soprano had to be flown out from England.

This reminds me of my earlier visits to Germany in 1974 to Duisburg when I sang with the renowned baritone, John Carol Case. Sensibly he always carried his Complan, a quick and easy nutrition, with him for sustenance. It was a performance I remember as well because in Bruckner's *Mass in A minor* I discovered during the rehearsal that there was a very small soprano solo I had not seen when studying the piece. Of course, I had to sight sing it during the rehearsal which was rather frightening. I certainly made sure that a similar situation never happened again.

Music festivals have a unique atmosphere of their own, with organisers buzzing around organising not only the concerts but social events. A joy to be part of them! I mention here three festivals which come to mind. In Germany at the Hitzacker Festival when I sang the part of Galatea in Handel's *Acis and Galatea*, "Heart, The Seat of Soft Delight", a glorious aria with cello obligato. I have warm memories of The Flanders Festival in Brugge with Christopher Hogwood and the Academy of Ancient Music performing J.S. Bach's *English Suites*. I was invited back the next year in Leuven, Belgium, taking one of the three sopranos in Handel's *Semele*. There was also the International Festival of Santander, a grand occasion. I sang often for the Three Choirs Festival in Gloucester, Hereford and Worcester but one performance sticks out in my mind, in my association with Michael Berkeley, Lennox Berkeley's son, who is also a composer. On the day before the first live performance of his new composition *Or shall we die?* the soprano was ill and I was asked by my agent if I would be willing to learn it overnight (this 20th century nightmare!) and perform it the next day. They could let me have the recent recording of it which they would send by special messenger. My husband Geoffrey and I spent the day and night learning it and listened to the recording all the way to the venue. I managed to give a performance where I felt the main criterion was to understand the text and convey its full meaning to the audience. It was very well received by the press. It is interesting that in this country we have one rehearsal of a performance on the day but abroad many days are allocated for rehearsals. Very often on the day of the performance there is no rehearsal at all so that everyone is well rested and fresh on the night.

Three of my wishes were to be the soloist in Beethoven's *Ninth Symphony*, to work with a fine conductor and to perform it many times. My wishes came true with the renowned Belgian conductor, André Vandernoot. I performed in 's-Hertogenbosch, Breda, Eindhoven and Tilburg in the Netherlands with the eminent bass, Jules Bastin, and in 1982 with the Philharmonic Orchestra at the Amsterdam Concertgebouw.

I must mention the Henry Wood promenade concerts at the Royal Albert Hall, where I appeared on nine occasions, two on the first nights from 1973 to 1982. Among them was the soprano role, Mater Gloriosa, in Mahler's *Eighth Symphony* with Pierre Boulez as conductor and the

Serenade to Music of Vaughan Williams with Andrew Davies as conductor. There was Bach's *Cantata 191* with Colin Davis, *A Midsummer Night's Dream* by Mendelssohn, conducted by Bernard Haitink, but the most memorable was when I was engaged to sing the part of Ascagne in *The Trojans* by Berlioz with Jessye Norman as Didon and Rozhdestvensky as conductor. A magnificent array of conductors! I shared the dressing room with Jesse Norman and we had some wonderful conversations. It was during the rehearsal of this work that the conductor and Jessye Norman, both very strong characters, did not see eye to eye on the interpretation of this piece. I think that when the conductor did not appear to take his bow with the soloists at the end of the performance, the audience must have noticed. However, Jessye Norman acting alone brought us all back on the stage for the usual bows to save the day. What should have been a wonderful occasion turned out to be an evening of considerable friction.

Another difficult experience as a singer is when one's emotions override control of the voice. This almost happened to me at St Martin-in-the-Fields when Benjamin Luxon and I performed at a memorial concert for the late Poet Laureate, Cecil Day-Lewis. It was a performance of the Fauré *Requiem* conducted by Meredith Davies. Sitting in the front row of the church was the poet's widow, the actress Jill Balcon, with the most pained expression I have ever experienced.

On a happier note, there was another concert with Meredith Davies somewhere in the north of England which escapes my memory at the moment when Meredith and Lennox Berkeley, the composer, needed a lift back to London and I felt quite honoured to be able to help such an eminent pair. They chatted happily in the back seat of the Audi car which I drove at the time. My association with the conductor, Meredith Davies, lasted many years from 1974 to 1985 when I performed with the Halle Orchestra at the Free Trade Hall in Manchester in performances of *Messiah* and Haydn's *Mass in D minor*; and also from 1977 with the Royal Choral Society at the Royal Albert Hall in five performances of *Messiah* for the Malcolm Sargent cancer fund for children. Meredith Davies had a close and celebrated association with Benjamin Britten and it was he who directed the première of the *War Requiem* in the newly restored Coventry Cathedral.

Meredith Davies next invited me to sing in a performance of the *War*

Requiem in South Africa. Geoffrey and I were on the second of two recital tours, travelling by car to the venues where we very much enjoyed the garden route from Durban to Cape Town. We were astonished to discover that one of the scenic attractions was a nudist colony, signposted en route before reaching the rehearsal venue for the *War Requiem*.

The first tour was simply a recital tour where Geoffrey and I gave recitals in Cape Town, Durban, Johannesburg and Stellenbosch for a recital to be recorded by the SABC. We were then invited for a tasting at the world-famous Stellenbosch vineyard where I did manage to buy two bottles of the delicious wine, wrapping them amongst my clothes very carefully in my case to take home. A crazy idea but on this occasion, it worked!

The songs for the recital programmes were chosen by Geoffrey very carefully. They were ones I longed to sing and that he longed to play. Strauss songs, of course, are my favourites. I began the recital with Strauss's *Morgen*, slow and sustained but with a lovely postlude beautifully played by Geoffrey. I also included songs by Mendelssohn, Chausson and Rachmaninov.

During my time in South Africa, I met a lady, Pansy, who was born in Redruth and knew my parents well. She said she wanted to introduce me to the Eathorne family in South Africa, whom she believed to be relations of mine. During the beginning of the nineteenth century many men from Cornwall went to South Africa to dig gold and earn money for their families at home and in fact many did not return. This was the case with my great-grandfather on Mummy's side, and Daddy's as well, I guess, since they were second cousins. He apparently had a great baritone voice and frequently sang heartily in the Four Lanes pub. Another good point was that he was very generous with his money and sent my great-grandmother enough to finance a house. The family in South Africa very much wanted to come to Four Lanes to meet my family there and so I mentioned this to my auntie and she said, "We don't want to know anything about that, Wendy." And so they never came. The saga still continues regarding connections with the extended family.

It was always a pleasure to be invited to France, as travelling there was quick and easy. I travelled to Paris in 1975 with the Cambridge Purcell Society in two performances of the Monteverdi *Vespers*. I was expecting Alice at the time and my thoughtful Cornish baritone, Richard Jackson, offered to help me with my case, for which I was grateful.

Regarding family matters, Geoffrey was not worried about having a child of our own but I certainly wanted one and if possible, a girl. I thought the ideal time would be when I was 35 or 36 so as not to leave it too late. I, of course, told Mummy about it and the reply was, "Well, you've done it now! No more peace for you. Don't say anything Wendy, but poor Mrs Orchard down the road is expecting too, poor soul!"

Of course, we remember that during the turn of the century, children during my parents' time were a problem for a lot of people having little money to support them. Now looking back on what I have written here, the baby from that poor soul got in touch with me a few weeks ago to tell me that her father's sister had died. She now lives in Canada with her husband and has an affluent life. How life changes!

Yes! Mummy adored Alice and sent me money each week for nappies. Daddy had already died but until she died Mummy did idolise Alice for four years. My delivery of the birth of Alice extended to midnight and I was asked if I would agree to a caesarean section operation so that the maternity team could go home. I, of course, after many hours in labour, agreed and my beautiful daughter Alice was born in the early morning of the 7th November 1975.

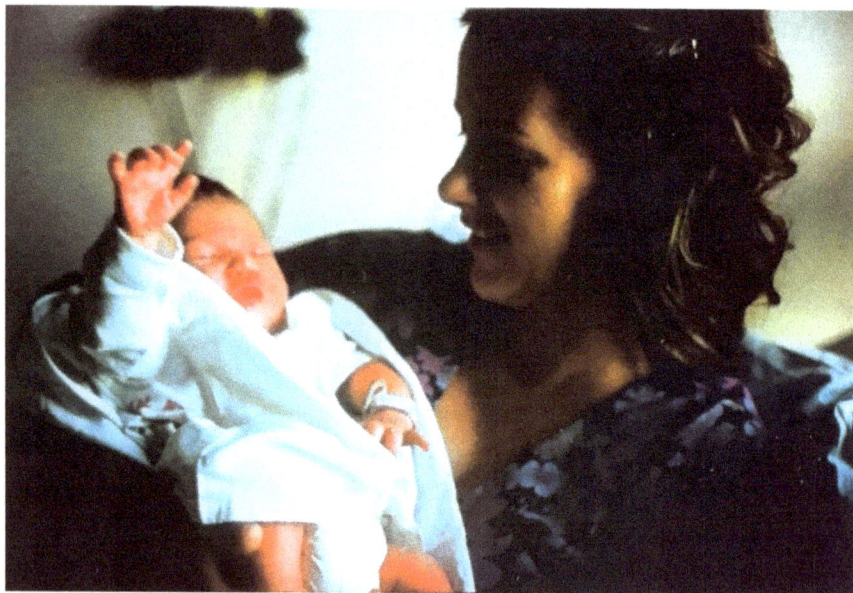

The day of Alice's birth at Queen Charlotte's Hospital in London

I returned to singing the Brahms *Requiem* three weeks later, which was not easy to sing with the opening, long soprano line. 'Ihr habt nun traurigkeit'. Sadly, I had to cancel the first BBC recording of a new modern piece and other concerts until the new year. After the birth of my daughter, Alice, I was extremely lucky to have a wonderful carer for her, a Mrs Clayton, who had much experience with young children. I located her through the Methodist Minister, the Reverend Cawffre, at the Ruislip Methodist Church where Alice was later baptised. Alice was extremely happy to bake cakes with Claytie, as we called her, which she enjoyed, I believe, most afternoons. As you can imagine, it was a tremendous bonus in my career to live with a wonderful accompanist also busy with his career and who was always available to help me. He continued to help three-year-old Alice when he taught her every day to play on a tiny violin with the result that she is today a very fine and busy violinist. She has two wonderful girls, Arabella and Ottilie, and with a very supportive husband, Laurence, she helps her musical daughters as her father did with her.

Alice as a professional violinist

Returning now to my career seems irrelevant when I want to tell you more about my daughter and grandchildren. Maybe later!

The performance of Mozart's *Coronation Mass* at Abbayes aux Hommes in 1979 was my introduction to the conductor, Jean-Pierre Dautel. I returned to work with the same conductor many times but one performance sticks out in my mind, not because of the performance of Bach Cantatas at Des Abbayes Normandes but during that day we were taken by a gentleman who had been on the beaches where the Second World War D-Day landings took place. He was able to give us detailed knowledge of that horrible time when according to him the Canadians were the strongest and most effective. On a happier note, we were taken to see the Bayeux Tapestry.

In 1978 the conductor, Richard Lowry, was keen to accompany me in a recital to be performed at the Théâtre de Caen. I chose a programme of Beethoven, Sibelius, Strauss and Elgar, since his work was little known in France at that time. I performed later with the conductor in two orchestral concerts in *Messiah* and Mozart's *Solemn Vespers*. In 1985 with l'Orchestre de Radio-France in Paris in three performances of Bach's *Mass in B Minor* with the conductor, Jean-François Paillard, in Montélimar, Valence and Grenoble. These concerts were to commemorate the tercentenary of Bach's birth. Before these concerts in France in late March, on March 20th the same year I flew off to Canada for a performance with the CBC Vancouver Orchestra of *St John Passion* with the conductor Jon Washburn, the director of the Vancouver Chamber Choir. It was not an easy concert with jet lag and what felt to be the middle of the night, in a dress which by that time was rather tight and uncomfortable. However, it made me think that to sing the second aria in *St John Passion* with its high tessitura I certainly did not need a fitted dress!

Talking of Canada reminds me of my promenade concert with the Toronto Mendelssohn Choir singing a Bach duet with John Elwes (*Cantata 191*) more than a decade earlier. A very comfortable evening I remember with the conductor, Colin Davis, who was ten years to the day older than I am.

There was always a dilemma between accepting concert or opera engagements, and I did feel that being offered the part of *Echo*, imitating the voice of Ariadne, would be a challenge in Strauss's *Ariadne auf Naxos*. It was at the Palermo Opera House in Sicily in April 1979, which would be my debut in Italy. There were eight performances and in all the five weeks there we only had five days of good weather. Strangely enough I was the only lady soloist in the cast not to be robbed. My husband, Geoffrey, brought Alice, who was then three and a half years old, over to

As Theophano with James Bowman as
Otto in Handel's Ottone *at the Sadler's*
Wells Theatre

Julia in 'La Vestale' by Spontini at
Birmingham's University Opera School

Almirena in Handel's opera Rinaldo *at*
Sadlers Wells Theatre with the Handel
Opera Society

Zerlina in Mozart's Don Giovanni *with*
Richard Van Allen as Don Giovanni for
the English National Opera at the
Coliseum

Sicily to visit me. We hired a car and visited Mount Etna, one of Europe's highest active volcanoes on the east coast of Sicily. Geoffrey and I took Alice to a rather lovely children's shop where we chose some dungarees and a T-shirt for her. The shop assistant's reaction was, "Bella bambina!" but Alice had different ideas and said, "No!"

She did not like what we had chosen so we took her around the shop and she chose a beautiful salmon pure silk dress which was far too large for her. We bought it at great expense but it was altered to suit her size over many years so that she could wear it, which she did as often as possible. I must say she looked delightful in it but the shopping day was rather spoilt when the assistant said, "Qual è tua nipote sembra adorabile!" (*"Your granddaughter looks beautiful!"*).

Alice in the apricot dress she chose

Alice did notice that one of the male soloists, *un maestro di danza* in the opera who particularly spoiled her, wore a wig and embarrassingly Alice was constantly trying to remove it! Thankfully she did enjoy calamari for her supper which distracted her.

It was a very hot day on the 23rd of September 1982 when I was invited to Cairo in Egypt to sing in Handel's *Alexander's Feast* to celebrate Saint Cecilia's Day. It was performed in the garden of the British Embassy in Cairo, surrounded on both sides by busy roads. In the evening performance it was obviously difficult for the audience to hear but apart from that in the afternoon and in the blazing heat the instrumentalists of the Sinfonia of Saint Bartholomew's were not prepared to rehearse with the chance of damaging their valuable instruments. This performance was also to celebrate the centenary of the Egypt Exploration Society and with the conductor, Robert Anderson, himself a qualified authority on the subject of ancient Egypt, who kindly took us to many exploration sites. What a fascinating experience! This was the first time that I had experienced a concert with a full orchestra singing in the open air. My host with whom I was staying during my visit said, "I couldn't hear a bloody thing. Do you make a living doing this sort of thing?"

However, I was taken back to their immaculate flat without them as they had a celebration that evening. There I found the Egyptian cook waiting to prepare me a meal which I declined, since I was not hungry after the flight. It certainly relieved him of his duties. Regretfully I heard the next day that while I had been left on my own the chorus had been given a wonderful party! At breakfast I was met by my host in his night attire and was served a breakfast of wonderful fresh mangoes. I awaited with great anticipation the arrival of the tenor, Kenneth Bowen, who was staying in the same apartment. The next day, a free one before travelling home, I was invited by the host and his young wife to lunch with their friends, which was most enjoyable. I was warned that it would be wise to wear something in silk because of the heat. I did have a dress in cool cotton which certainly did the trick for me but not before my hostess mentioned that she did not think it would be suitable. What could I say?

On to Spain and Santander! Wow! What a lovely place and how fortunate to be invited in 1990 to the 30th International Festival of Santander to sing in two performances, one of the Mozart *Requiem* and the other of *Messiah*. Who could resist a swim there? The tenor, Peter Jeffes, and I managed to do so between the two performances. I'm afraid Santander in Spain was the first place to spring to mind but I shouldn't forget that in 1983 I visited Gerona in Italy singing in Handel's *Dixit Dominus* and Fauré's *Requiem*, and the same programme again in Barcelona at the Paulau de La Musica Catalana, one of the most recommended tourist attractions of Barcelona. My first performance in Spain in 1977 was with the conductor, Neville Marriner, with the Academy of Saint Martin in the Fields at Antiqua Iglesias de Los PP

Paules in Cuenca singing in two performances of Handel's *Israel in Egypt*. Even though we were often treated to wonderful meals when travelling to different countries, the Barcelona occasion sticks out in my mind because it was in an elegant oak-panelled room where we were served the most luscious meal perhaps unwisely just before the performance. I shared it with my close friends, the tenor Neil MacKie and his wife Kathleen Livingstone, who were also appearing that evening. Luckily it did not have an adverse effect on any of us.

Going to Scotland for me was always a treat, not only because of the many performances at Haddo House or with the Royal Scottish National Orchestra and conductor, Sir Alexander Gibson, but for the picturesque journey from Euston by rail to Scotland which at times is breathtaking. At Haddo House as the soprano soloist I was given the honour of sleeping in the Queen's bedroom with its silk sheets. I am sad and ashamed to say that I did tear them with my clumsy size three foot. One particular performance sticks out in my mind, of Honneger's rarely performed *King David*, with Kenneth Baker, the BBC newsreader, as narrator. On another occasion at Haddo House Lady Aberdeen arranged for the four soloists to have tea with the Queen Mother. We were told that as soon as the Queen Mother finished eating, we should also stop. As a result, we only enjoyed just one tiny, delicious cucumber sandwich. The men rather hogged the conversation on the subject of architecture but I do remember one comment she made, which was, "No lady now should marry a man who can't cook!"

A performance at The Royal Festival Hall of Serenade to Music *by Vaughan Williams where I met Queen Elizabeth and Prince Charles*

CHAPTER SEVEN

Magistrates

✸

Perhaps I should tell you how, after being a musician all my life, I became a magistrate. Not being a great reader, I have always instead observed people's characters with enormous interest.

While watching the television news one day I noticed that a magistrate had been very helpful in giving advice on a particular aspect of law. The year was 1988 and having had an incredible solo career I was interested in finding something new I could have as an added interest. But how was I to deal with this? Of course, where else but the Citizens Advice Bureau in Ruislip, where I was living. So I walked down past the duckpond to the Bureau building and waited my turn to speak to an adviser. I learned that I needed two sponsors to recommend me and hopefully if I was a suitable candidate I would be given an opportunity to meet with the magistrates committee who would assess my suitability. Of course, I discussed this with Michael, who wasn't at all sure if he wished to live with a magistrate, but when the closing date was approaching for my application and I needed an answer, he said, "Well, if you want to do it, get on with it."

Now my problem was which two sponsors to approach. My two choices became clear. Dame Janet Baker, a great friend and colleague, was more than happy to accommodate and Meredith Davies, the Principal of Trinity College of Music, was someone I had worked with a great deal as a singer, when he was the most wonderful conductor. His comment was, "Wendy, I wanted to be a magistrate but it didn't happen."

I waited patiently for a reply and eventually after a few weeks was called for a meeting which would be of an hour's duration and where I would need to have made myself acquainted with some aspects of law. Naturally I did some research and discovered that all criminal cases begin in a magistrates' court, where they pass the most serious crimes to the Crown Court. Magistrates deal with less serious criminal cases such as minor theft, criminal damage, public disorder, motoring offences and common assault, not causing significant injury. They can grant licensing of premises and most magistrates will, I'm sure, have spent many hours on the bench listening to and discussing why licence fees have not been paid, in particular TV and car licensing.

The meeting was serious and to the point! Their first question was, "Please give us one reason why you think we should choose you as a magistrate?"

I replied, "I think that I have a balanced mind."

They then read me a court case and asked me what sentence I would give.

I said, "Could you tell me the choices I have?"

The answer came back, "A custodial sentence, a conditional discharge, community work, etc."

I must have satisfied the committee as a few weeks later I was granted a position as a magistrate. I was one of the 40% granted to sit at Feltham and Brentford. This was not in my home area, as there were already too many middle-class, middle-aged Christian ladies there. The Feltham Courthouse held a stately room with a big oak table, with magistrates for Court 1, the chairman and one winger sitting each side of the chairman. In this most stately atmosphere, I was only brave enough to be a winger, but this did not prevent me from having an individually strong opinion when required, although the advice of the clerk was extremely valuable and taken very seriously. It was a new, different and incredible experience where we had many weeks of training with the "singing" Clerk. It was his singing, of course, which interested me. He apparently just loved it as an amateur. He explained everything explicitly with examples, questions and answers and divided us into groups on different cases where the answers from the groups often varied. As I recall there was no dress code to sit at court but suits for the men and women were appropriate. I believe the women wore hats originally and so later in the hot summer months it came as a bit of a shock when I was greeted one day with, "Nice to see you today in your pyjamas, Wendy!"

Like Mrs Thatcher I was undeterred.

In the retiring room after a case where we were first given advice and procedure from the Justices' Clerk the three of us magistrates would discuss it in detail. My colleagues would often end up with an entirely different decision from that at first anticipated.

My very first sitting was with two male magistrates when we had to discuss magazines hidden on the top shelves in newsagents and whether or not they were too sexually explicit to exhibit. I glanced through these magazines for a while and then said that I was ready to retire to discuss it. A quick reply from my colleagues was that I must read the small print and so after quite a considerable time we retired to discuss it. I remember being quite shocked by the contents and as far as I can remember permission was not granted.

As already mentioned all criminal cases begin in a magistrates' court which deals with the less serious cases. Magistrates can decide on bail, for example. They must have certain qualities in order to become magistrates. These are sound judgement, maturity, commitment and reliability, social awareness, understanding, communication and good character. They must not, of course, have a criminal record.

CHAPTER EIGHT

Teaching

✳

As a teacher, it never dawned on me that I would one day be flying to
Hong Kong for that very purpose. It was a very adventurous time.
We were on the runway when all I could see was the ocean. No one had
mentioned that the runway was shorter than most, but nonetheless, we
arrived safety. The hotel was very comfortable and on my first night, there
was a surprise knock on the door.

"Could you immediately go downstairs – small problem. Hotel on
fire!" On the 9th floor I walked slowly behind some elderly ladies down
the stairs. Oh, I do now sympathise with the ladies in their senior years,
being one myself. There was a small fire in the kitchen, so it seemed, and
I in my night attire in the hot night thought it best to venture to the next
hotel for breakfast, which I did. It was a long wait before returning early
morning to my hotel and with jet lag and an early start the next day I felt
rather gloomy.

It was good to meet Michael Rippon, an RAM colleague and fine
singer, the acting present Head of Music at The Performing Arts
Conservatoire, where I was about to teach. I had a most interesting and
rewarding time with the students and a social evening was arranged the
next day, except there was a typhoon warning. It was prohibited to go out
of the hotel. Most evenings I could not sleep but as luck would have it, I
enjoyed some rather good programmes on television. My experience
gave me no inclination to return and in future I would stay in England
and accept invitations to teach, adjudicate and examine at Charter House
School, Benslow, and in major music colleges in Britain.

My early teaching started when I was in my first year at the Royal
Academy and I was rather pleased that my cousin Margaret, who lived
opposite in Four Lanes, the village where I lived and in fact was born, had

a pretty voice. I offered to teach her the first song I was taught at the Academy, purely for pronunciation, without the curdled "u" sound and overstretched "r's" might I add. Miss Blyth, my teacher, had to use her best teaching skills to help me through the Cornish accent. We laughed a lot in the process.

This was done as in my junior school, where a slap of the leg was normal if I got things wrong. Poor Margaret had to endure the same approach but to pay me back for such treatment she put her cat on my back. I am terrified of animals and so it was indeed a huge punishment which I rightly deserved. Living opposite, my Auntie Florie, my godmother, also made a comment, "Do you have to practise singing at 10pm? My dear Wendy, we're all asleep by 9pm!"

My teaching did progress as I was asked by the Academy to take over a vacancy at a Bethnal Green School for the Inner London Education Authority, teaching geography and music, mostly singing. The students loved singing and did so with gusto and tremendous energy. One day when I arrived at the classroom for geography the students were all sitting on the floor giggling, but when they tried to get up for the lesson, I announced that no, we were having it on the floor. Not so amusing then.

Teaching then vanished for a while as I spent a great deal of time learning how to teach within the art of professional singing, of which I knew nothing. Dr Weymouth, Musical Director at the Grammar School, had said, "Wendy, I know nothing about the art of professional singing but I can select suitable songs for you to sing." We certainly enjoyed working together.

On leaving the RAM after six years I was in demand as a teacher but sadly only had time to take on a few students. One in particular was Mary Weigold, who is now a wonderful singer, songwriter and teacher at Trinity Laban Conservatoire of Music and Dance. To see me for her lessons in London she had regularly travelled down from Durham. Life continued with so many singing engagements that my agent informed me that many colleagues benefited from my not being available to accept more than one at the same time. By the late 80s my desire to teach again came into fruition when Meredith Davies, a distinguished conductor with whom I had often worked as a singer, invited me to teach at Trinity College of Music, where he was the principal. David

Pettit, chief administrator at the time, gave me three second-study singers, with half an hour a week each to teach. I guess he felt I had a lot to learn before throwing me in at the deep end, and how right he was. The students were delightful and despite being naturally more interested in their first study than singing, settled down well. I certainly hope that I projected a keen interest in teaching as the moment had arrived to fulfil my ambition to be as good a teacher as a performer. It really does take a term, at least, to feel comfortable as personalities working together and for students to briefly understand the art of singing and how the teaching of it progresses over four years. I somehow felt that I was much helped by joining *The Association of Teachers of Singing* and *The Association of English Singers and Speakers* where we all met and chatted about our own ideas, helped by refreshments, of course! We all agreed that to be able to speak with clarity and direction is of major importance because out of that comes the start of involvement and a focus on effective dramatic intention.

The last most interesting seminars I attended were at the Voice Clinic of the Ferens Institute at the Middlesex and Devonshire Hospitals in London. It was scary! Pictures on screen were viewed with the entire working of the larynx displayed.

"We need a volunteer to give us all an insight as to how it works," the organiser announced. My head immediately dropped but a young man desperately keen to make use of every opportunity raised his hand and there he was with a camera down his throat while we all watched. I have to say that I have never given the larynx a minute's thought when singing but there are specialists to elaborate and singers keen to listen. They find that knowing how the larynx works can be very useful when singing. Back to how we teach – or should I say the way I teach, as we teachers are all so different, each with our own style of teaching. I have a system of symbols which I use for the positioning of vowels and consonants. I suggest facial movements supported by what has to be correct breath control to make words clear and precise together with a good, well produced vocal sound. I will do my best to explain in the appendix.

All this can take more than the four-year course at college but if it has progressed well the Postgraduate Course may be suggested. In my case the Academy kindly offered me a scholarship to continue studying. I was so lucky! However few students attending colleges become viable as professional singers and indeed realise early on that they cannot commit themselves to such detailed study. They work hard enough to pass exams and attain a degree, all of which makes me very happy as long as they are happy. It can be frustrating, however, for a teacher if the student's voice is exceptionally beautiful yet ambition is lacking, or if the student is lazy and has to be motivated somehow. In fact, there are so many reasons why so few students become professional singers and why only one or two, or fewer make the grade each year.

However, for me after five years of progressing and being given many more students to teach – first study students – the post of first Head of Vocal Studies was advertised and I applied for the job. At this point Meredith Davies had retired and I received a phone call one evening from Philip Jones, the new principal, offering me the new post as Head of Vocal Studies. I was delighted but knew that this was to be an enormous task and attaining the post needed much preparation before facing, as I remember, a panel of four.

"Wendy, what ideas do you have to enhance the running of the singing department?"

I was prepared. My answers came thick and fast.

"Let's offer exchange student courses with music colleges abroad."

"The department would appreciate a pianist solely for them."

"Let's offer a talented postgraduate a financial post at the college each year."

"Let's have a party and invite directors, managers and celebrities to hear very talented students with a view to mentoring."

"Students having completed their studies always find it very difficult to promote themselves. They need help with letter writing, dressing appropriately, etiquette within presentation."

I remember when training the next Head of Vocal Studies, the celebrated Linda Hirst, and feeling strongly about presentation, I mentioned, "If you see a student untidily dressed for an audition or examination you can say to yourself this singer is going to be a mess."

To which Linda replied, "Oh Wendy, how can you say that?"

"Easily," I said. Five years or so later Linda conceded, "I take your point!"

The first day I arrived at Trinity College of Music in Mandeville Place, London WI as the new Head of Vocal Studies I was directed into a room next to the secretary's room where the efficient Beryl maintained a steely watch, occasionally bringing in a few packets of mail. The Head of Strings, Derek Aviss, later to become principal of the college and who indeed had been a student many years previously, arrived and was as helpful as he could be. Next was the Head of Piano, the wonderful pianist John Bingham, who had no intention of becoming an administrator and so happily walked the corridors smoking constantly. He could, however, remember everything that was said at meetings while the rest of us had to search through our notes feeling somewhat inadequate. Finally, there was the Head of Wind, Stephen Nagy, a very amusing character but like John, rarely seen in the office.

Gradually we found our way by inviting new staff to teach, etc. It was, however, far from easy when one of the staff informed me that there was a petition by the staff to try and oust me. This really upset me but when I considered, realising that the other applicants had been members of Trinity College long before me, with much more experience, I did understand the situation. Nonetheless I rang the principal, Philip Jones, who assured me that his word was paramount.

I was terrified of chairing our first staff meeting, where the atmosphere was somewhat icy, but was immediately cheered when eyeing my lovely friend, the distinguished tenor, John Wakefield, who had been a Glyndebourne colleague. I certainly knew that a few bottles of wine would sweeten the atmosphere. Tessa Cahill also appeared. She was the glamorous soprano noted for her many roles at Covent Garden and we had met at Glyndebourne in the chorus where Jani Strasser only chose exceptional singers to grace the stage.

Staff and students have one thought. Am I being appreciated and should I be given more students to teach?

An example of one student's question, "What major operatic role will I be given this year?" to which I replied, "But you had the major role last year."

"Yes, but what about me this year?"

These were not my major problems but it was challenging being involved in the new Honours Degree, for evaluation by the University of

Westminster with its vocational music, and also being module leader for the singing department. This involved meeting and cooperating with module leaders of the other departments, creating a new course which was interesting and challenging for the students, covering two main areas, performance studies and applied professional studies. I now had to present stage work so my title progressed to Head of Vocal Studies, Opera and Music Theatre.

Before expanding on Opera and Music Theatre I will give you some brief information on the four yearly levels of one-to-one teaching.

Level One:
Introducing vocal technique and in particular breath control and posture. As repertoire we worked on Italian Aria Antique or English Song introducing our first foreign language. Good musicianship was vital and I was constantly checking phrasing intonation and clarity of words. I had to be aware of the student's character and together aim for confidence and trust as a partnership.

Level Two:
I instructed how to build a vocal technique, adding German Lieder as development of another language. Interpretation of songs or arias was always discussed. I might suggest an operatic aria for future stage work where appropriate or an aria from an oratorio for church services.

I proposed the students listen to vocal music particularly to make personal choices of repertoire and by listening in order to become aware of different styles. It was encouraging if students chose their own repertoire but I was asked if I would like to suggest suitable songs for auditions and so forth. Two volumes of my Audition Songs were published by Kevin Mayhew in 2004.

Level Three:
One is constantly building vocal technique and at this level adding the French language, which can be much more tricky to master. The French language became my favourite language to sing in but not before a lot of hard work. We discussed presenting programmes with the fourth-year recital in mind and talked about stage techniques.

Level Four:
I would have expected by now a secure technique with much colouring of words and presenting a variety of different songs and arias for the all-important final recital. We might have a trial run at my home, making it more of a social occasion. Having a pool in the garden used to mean that on a hot day a bikini seemed a much cooler prospect to wear for the final recital! The venue of Saint Mary's Church, Perivale, with an invited audience to offer advice to the student performers was a more sober occasion and only after the exams at college did celebration wine flow.

The pool has been great fun for everyone

Little did I know that by myself I would be arranging the whole Postgraduate Course:

There were two years now to work on advanced vocal technique in the music chosen, presenting detailed work on interpretation of songs and arias in the many languages and styles chosen. The performance had to capture the attention of an audience for the final Master's Degree recital. That entailed the student having excellent communication with his or her teacher, receiving encouragement for good progress, with understanding and sympathy when required. Having extra performance opportunities was also very helpful.

Returning to Opera and Music Theatre, as a performance study I selected an opera each year to be in an external venue as the college's annual production. One year I suggested a composition by Dr Anton Tučapský, a teacher at the college. It was an opera *The Undertaker*, a challenging contemporary and adventurous new work for students to experience. I assessed students suitable for particular parts depending on their ability as performers and actors and at the same time considering the need to give all students opportunities to perform as part of the educational process. Suitable venues, directors, producers and builders had to be chosen to stage the annual production. Prior to the first rehearsal of *The Undertaker* passers-by were bemused to see a procession of coffins being carried into the Rudolf Steiner Hall!

It was stranger still to be approached by a student one day to say that one of the teachers could be viewed taking part in the notorious video series, *Lovers' Guide*. I thought perhaps that I should discuss it with the principal, which I duly did. He suggested that I needed to prove the fact by getting the video. Asking in Blockbusters, a nearby video rental shop, my partner, Michael, was embarrassed to be told, "Oh no, sir. We don't keep that sort of thing here!" but as he was just on the point of leaving a low voice added, "I think you will find it at our Hayes branch." And indeed, that turned out to be the case. As it happened the principal did not have a VHS video player so he asked me to inform him of the content and if in fact the allegation was true. After I had viewed the episode in question I answered as best I could, but was never informed what action was subsequently taken. What I do know is that the students were gleefully showing the video as a fun piece at all their parties.

This is a chapter which combines different aspects of teaching: how it is viewed, how it is taught and how we love to listen to music with open minds at all the different stages of teaching. It leads up to Trinity Laban's Annual Gold Award Ceremony, performed each year with the best students chosen by each Head of Department. The overall winner is chosen to receive the highly regarded Gold Medal. What a perfect opportunity this was to attend each year with the primary idea of inviting these extremely talented soloists to appear in my next concert venture, *Stars of Trinity Laban*.

CHAPTER NINE

Stars of Trinity Laban

✺

Now living on the south coast with time to spare, I was approached by the chairman of the Lymington Choral Society for ideas on how she could next entertain the choir members at their annual party. This was a serious thought for me! My students long to perform and this would be a grand opportunity for them. Obviously to come from London with their accompanist would incur costs. I informed Shirley, the chairman, of my proposal. I in fact had three sopranos, Rebekah, Daisy and Suen, at that time who could sing "Three Little Maids from School" from *The Mikado* and they would love to have this chance to perform their solo exam pieces for later in the year as well. Would this work? Shirley was delighted and so we put our heads together and presented "*A Musical Soirée*" with wine and canapés. It was greatly appreciated and even made a financial profit after all expenses were paid, leaving half for the choir. The wonderful professional pianist, Paul Chilvers, was extremely generous with his fee and the singers' expenses were covered. I prepared a packed picnic for the train back to London. The chocolate cake they still remember! This was performed on 23rd July 2014.

The question now was, did I want this to progress? So many ideas then raced through my mind with the result that *Stars of Trinity Laban* was formed. Could I possibly include not just singers but all the different faculties of Trinity Laban to make performances totally varied and more interesting to more people? Different friends kept giving me new ideas and problems. Which venue should we choose in Lymington? Daphne Johnston, who was at the same time setting up a new project, *The Solent Festival*, informed me that St Thomas' Church was the prime venue for concerts in the area. I followed her advice, but it was expensive.

"How will you finance it, Wendy?" was the burning question. I resolved to set up a new bank account with £1000 to underwrite it. Might Trinity Laban help in some way? They certainly did, by producing all the printed material and putting me in touch with the excellent students that I heard and so enjoyed watching perform at the Gold Award Ceremony. How about an audience? The Lymington Choral Society were my greatest connection and Shirley, the chairman, made sure that all members of the choir were informed by means of my cousin Vivien Parsons, the Publicity Trustee, who researched every venue. Audiences were not a problem; in fact, on one occasion there was a full house. On another occasion I had the idea that I would set up the concert in the round. This was an intriguing enhancement of another great evening for the audience. The vicar at the time, Peter Salisbury, apparently thought the idea was such a good one that he might use the same arrangement himself some time. Travel from London? This was sponsored by South Western Railway on one occasion after an idea given to me by one of my daughter's friends, Lucy. Advertising in this area? *The Lymington Times* is a very popular newspaper as is the *Lymington Directory*. By no means least of all was the assistance of a very successful prize-winning photographer, William Bonett, who so kindly came to all the concerts. He took splendid photographs of all the performers, one of which was always printed in *The Lymington Times* together with a review.

The Mayor congratulating the artists at St Thomas' Church, Lymington

I set about finding new venues in this area in which to perform. The Forest Arts in New Milton would be ideal, with a theatre space not too big and extremely accessible. I arranged a meeting with the manager, who offered me a generous sum to put on a concert. Naturally I was overjoyed but I needed to select programmes more suited to the venue. Sam Jewison was a very talented piano and tenor student at the time at Trinity Laban and a specialist in *The Great American Songbook*. He seemed the ideal person to present this performance, and suggested we call the programme *Showtime Greats*. One of my students, Rebekah Smith, soprano, could join Sam, with Stefan Melovski, a guitarist I had chosen for the evening. Among the numbers were "I Get a Kick Out of You" and "Anything Goes" by Cole Porter. It was a great evening with an excellent box-office. One particular gentleman admired him so much he wanted to buy shares in Sam of which not surprisingly none existed at the time. He requested that Sam came with his orchestra for *The Solent Festival*. Sam certainly performed on many further occasions for Stars of Trinity Laban and as a one-man show recently did so for *The Solent Festival*.

More Magic of the Musicals
STARS OF TRINITY LABAN

Sam Jewison - Vocalist and Pianist
Daniele Nastri – Soprano
Harry Evans – Trumpet and Double Bass
Produced by Wendy Eathorne

Forest Arts Centre
Saturday 2 November, 7.30pm

Each year from 2014 I presented interesting programmes in my recital series. I introduced many instrumentalists and various pianists. Yuko Yagishiti from Japan was later awarded the unusual privilege and permission to perform in countries around the world. A Japanese violinist, Tadasuke Iljlma, was a first-prize winner in many prestigious competitions including the highest award in Tokyo *New Stars of Music Competition*. There was Urska Horvat, a young Slovenian cellist, winner of the *TEMSIG National Competition* (Slovenian), *Wettbewerb für Violoncello Liezen* (Austria) and *Young International Janigro Competition* (Croatia). The Spanish flautist, Ana Estefania Rodriguez Moran, has been awarded twice the *AIE* (Spanish Performers Competition for young outstanding musicians), and is part of the Duo Villanesco with guitar. Naturally I cannot mention all the performers. but suffice to say that they were all chosen from the Gold Award for their expertise and were greatly appreciated, particularly by the Lymington Town Mayor who gave an impromptu speech. They did look wonderful in their finery! The programme I believe was rather special including: Tzigane – Ravel (Violin); Fiancailles pour rire (Soprano); Ballade No1 in G minor Op 23 (Piano) and On this Island, Op 11, Britten (Soprano).

I was aware that Beaulieu Abbey was a wonderful venue at which to perform, and Philip Daish Handy was the local fine musician who selected artists to perform at the Abbey. How delighted I was when Philip gave me a date for *Stars of Trinity Laban*! It was Armistice Day, 11th November 2017. I had to choose the programme. My immediate thought was that we should have a speaker join us. I asked the distinguished contemporary soprano Linda Hirst, Head of Vocal Studies, if she could suggest someone suitable. By chance one of the Chamber Choir at college was a vicar and he agreed to think and come back with ideas. He did come back but later wondered if I could release him since he was invited to meet the bishop on several important matters. Of course, I agreed as I have been in such dilemmas myself. Always difficult though! At short notice I thought the only thing I could do was to hope that my partner, Michael Goldthorpe, an English graduate from Cambridge, would be able to produce something interesting in the time available, which he did grandly.

The concert at Beaulieu Abbey on Armistice Day

What more is there to say about the *Stars of Trinity Laban*? In all we did eleven performances, each time with different artists and different programmes in three different venues. It was sad that we could not continue. We had booked one performance in June 2019 at St Thomas' Church and another in 2020. Yuko was to come back in 2020 by request of Beaulieu Abbey Church, who were keen for us to return, as was the generous lady who financed our concert. Needless to say, the Covid-19 lockdown was the cause of these cancellations.

CHAPTER TEN

My Life Now

❋

I have previously mentioned Michael, my partner, also a singer. We first met in Sunderland when I was married to Geoffrey and Michael to Gill, but only in 1983 did we meet again in Germany, when we both were having marital problems. We have been together now for just under forty years and been blessed with five children between us. Alice, my daughter, and Michael's children Alice, Emily, Ben and Stephen.

Michael and I out exercising on our tandem

Unfortunately, Michael fell down the stairs in 2020 with resulting serious injuries and my major job now is as the main carer for him. Ben and Stephen, who both live in England, do help when they can but Alice and Emily both live far away, in Australia and America respectively. They visit when possible. Being a village girl, I have found it easy to adapt and Michael and I have a schedule which we enjoy. A good cook-carer, Nyree, who makes us delicious rice pudding amongst other tasty goodies, helps me with the making of the Christmas cake. I do somewhat suffer with scoliosis, sadly, but in Lymington, Hampshire, where we live there are many pleasures to be had, one of which is the Lymington Choral Society, where Michael was the conductor and Artistic Director before his fall. The Solent Music Festival provides a week of wonderful music run by the eminent pianist, Sam Haywood, and organised by Daphne Johnson, who is very much a live wire in the town. She also arranges the Christmas Tree Festival each December with trees brought by local organisations. They are decorated by them and are displayed at the church before being sold, the money made then being given to various charities.

Michael and me after his accident

My 80th Birthday Celebration at the Royal Festival Hall

The 80th family party at Alice's home with Alice, Arabella and Ottilie

With Alice on her Graduation Day

My daughter, Alice, her husband, Laurence and my precious granddaughters, Arabella, 13 and Ottilie, 10, come to see us every three weeks from London, where they live. Both Michael and I look forward so much to seeing them and of course they all spoil us. Previously, when we lived in Ruislip I entertained my friends and family as much as possible and of course the pool we had in the garden was a winner. Coming from Cornwall I really wanted the luxury of a pool and Geoffrey agreed as long as a Steinway piano was forthcoming for him. Of course it was. Geoffrey helped me very much with my career and chose all my music for my recital work, arranging the many competitions for me in Britain and abroad. Why demur from working together with the luxury of a Steinway piano! We separated amicably and Geoffrey chose as his new wife, Vija, who later had a daughter, Stephanie, a new step-sister for Alice. Michael invited Geoffrey as pianist for an all-Beethoven programme, at which Alice also played, in St Thomas' Church. Alice loved her father so much and after he died arranged a big Memorial Concert for him in London at St George's Church, Hanover Square. Alice has so many connections from the Royal College of Music, where she studied, and has had experience in the various genres from classical to pop and heavy metal, not to mention all the musical arrangements, recordings, teaching and orchestral playing she undertakes. I can only scratch the surface of the amount of work my wonderful Alice packs into her life. The memorial concert was an enormous success as Geoffrey was immensely kind to everyone and was accepted as an exceptionally fine musician. The money donated for the concert is to go to the Parkinson's Disease charity. She did so kindly take me for my 70th birthday to New York, where we saw *Madame Butterfly* at the Metropolitan Opera House and had dinner in between the acts, which was something I had always wanted to do.

In New York at the Metropolitan Opera House

Our musical family had to continue in some way and of course there is Alice and her husband, Laurence, who has no mean baritone voice when he chooses to let us hear it. He greatly supports Alice and the children and, for instance, was a great help by formatting the programme for the memorial concert. He always keeps a keen eye on his two daughters' progress and loves to listen to them play and sing. Arabella is now considering a diploma on the violin after achieving a distinction in grade 8 violin. From age seven Anabella has had piano lessons and will take grade 8 shortly. She also improvises on the guitar. She has singing lessons, which were requested by the conductor of her choir at Notting Hill School in Ealing. Ottilie at the same school plays the clarinet, the piano, sings in the school choir and following a recent request for her birthday, plays the drums. Ottie has two Grade 5s and will have another before she is 11. Both girls swim for Ealing and are extremely good. Alice has been approached regarding Ottilie's continuing to a much higher level but because of her school work the hours required make it impossible. As Alice's mother I can truly say what joy Alice brings to our lives. Like her father she is always there to help and a huge support, now that my health is so tiresome with painful Scoliosis and other little nuisances that seem to appear. Alice was born in the seventies, during which time I more or less missed out on Alice's young years because of my career. Now as their grandmother I am proud to say that my great joy has been looking after the girls when required by Alice while she pursues her very busy career. When we moved from Ruislip, Alice suggested we live near her so we were lucky to find a house in Acton Town, about a mile from Alice and Laurence. At the same time Michael and I bought a house in Lymington, where we live now on the coast, to accommodate my passion for swimming. I was never taught to swim and once when I complained about this while on the beach for "tea-treat", an outing arranged by the Methodist church, my mother answered, "What is wrong with you? Get into the sea and don't come out until you can swim!" That I did, but my swimming technique is laughable. When I swim with the girls they watch tentatively, in order to rescue me if necessary. I certainly made sure that Alice was taught and she is a fantastic swimmer with enormous breath control, hence her being chosen to take a class of synchronised swimmers. It was during my trips to Beaconsfield for Alice's swimming that my friend, Josephine, invited me to her party, where I met Judy Norman, who has become a firm and lasting friend, attending as many of my London concerts as she could. When I was so busy with my career, Alice was very happy with her older carer, Mrs Clayton (Claytie), who was recommended by the Minister of the Methodist Church in Ruislip where we lived at the time. We were blessed to have Claytie who loved Alice dearly. I do have Michael's family, Ben

I loved to swim

and his wife, Rehmah, originally from Uganda, who makes us two-portion meals of spicy treats and my favourites for the freezer. She often brings brownies when she comes to see us en route from her work with autistic and troubled children. Towards this work she has already put on highly successful charity evenings supporting *The Blossom Development Trust* at Le Palais Des Vaches in Exbury. This trust helps children and young people with special needs on their journey towards independence, self-worth and a fulfilling happy life. Ben and Rehmah have three offspring, Michel, 22, Tyler, 18 and Leilani, 14, who are all paving their way towards exciting careers. They are so helpful to Michael and me when they come to see us as often as they can. Stephen, his younger son, has an interesting life, for certain periods working hard and then traveling. He sees himself moving eventually to India. Meanwhile he lives about a two-hour drive away in Roehampton but comes to see us around every four weeks. I wanted very much to see the play *The Crucible* in London so Stephen kindly took me. Ben drove me to attend Geoffrey's Memorial Concert which Dame Janet attended, as did all our family, including Laurence's mother, Ruth, and his sister, Isabel. Geoffrey had been Dame Janet's pianist for many years. We travelled many miles to concerts together when Alice and I were invited. I invited Dame Janet Baker as a famous singer to inspire the students on a day of celebration.

Michael's family celebration at Burley Manor

As you have seen we have two Alices in the family. Michael's Alice was born in 1969 and my daughter in 1975. Alice has three offspring in Australia, a boy and twin girls with Alan, her first husband. Then with her second husband, Lucon, she acquired a ready-made family of eight more! Michael's younger daughter, Emily, had five children with her first husband, Darran, and acquired two more who lived with her second husband, Arley. It was two years after Michael's fall that he decided to get all the family together for a celebration, especially since in any event his daughter Alice was coming to England to meet her new husband's family in Luton. The celebration was held in Burley Manor on a hot day in May, a grand occasion as we all believed that Michael would not live to a great age considering the severity of the fall. We had a wonderful time and after almost five years Michael is still here and improving all the time. We have many special friends here in Lymington due to Michael's luck in having so many opportunities to which he could apply when arriving in 2006. He became the conductor and artistic director of the Lymington Choral Society and a singing tutor for Priestlands School.

Rebecca Millington, a member of the choir, introduced Michael to David Rule, a funder for the choir and later I met his partner, Sandra. We have good times socially as we do with Ron and Celia. The latter were introduced to me by my colleague at Trinity Laban, Linda Hirst. Both Ron and Linda's husband, Gillian, are retired clergymen and Celia, a Doctor of Economics. Celia had briefly met my friends, Valerie and Chris Isham, who are in the same line of work, so I thought it apt to invite Valerie to join our parties where they could share memories in common. What was unusual among our other friends was that out of the blue, Denis Rothwell contacted Michael, introducing himself as a long-lost second cousin. Michael was surprised and delighted to see Denis after an interval of more than sixty years. I was aware that my cousins, Janice and Trevor, lived nearby in Chandlers Ford and her sister, Vivien, and David in Hythe. We were all born in the same village and at Christmas played hide and seek when no one could find them in their sprawling house.

There were always occasions to go back to Cornwall. I bought a small flat in Truro in order to be independent for the many visits as a Trustee for the Hall for Cornwall and as a Bard where ceremonies were held in

At a Bardic Ceremony in Penzance

different parts of Cornwall. I was a patron of the Duchy Opera and enjoyed so many wonderful performances where many talented singers in Cornwall were able to show off their prowess. Naturally I used the opportunity to visit the family. Kathryn, my cousin, organised a secret family gathering for me at the Carlyon Hotel which gave me a wonderful surprise and an opportunity to meet the extended family.

More recently my cousin, Charmaine, set about organising a photographic party at the Penventon Hotel, replicating what happened many years ago. She organised food when the hotel served Cornish food and much more. Being unable to travel was a problem but Charmaine and her husband Bryan drove from Cornwall to Lymington to take me there and back. I desperately wanted to attend and was so delighted the problem was solved, thanks to their very generous offer. I met Malcolm my older cousin and his wife Janice and their daughter, Sharon, who when she visits her daughter in Hampshire always visits Michael and me. David, Malcolm's brother, and his wife Daphne used to organise the Truro Music Festival. One year I was invited to judge. After the adjudication I was firmly reprimanded by a lady who was cross that I had written about her daughter that singing was not for her. There was good reason but I guess it was cruel and I won't be that tough again!

A party with my family at the Penventon Hotel

Annabella Waite, a singer and teacher friend of mine, was very much involved in the inauguration of the Duchy Opera, of which I am a patron, and more recently in acquiring the wonderful new piano for the Cathedral. Michael and I were invited to the opening concert for the piano. Annabella's joy is to come to Lymington to the Solent Music Festival with us.

Some years ago, Michael was awarded a scholarship to explore and promote Victorian and Edwardian Music. This led to the formation of The Bold Balladiers, where I was Special Adviser and Michael, Musical Director. He organised many concert visits to care homes and schools all over England, Scotland and Wales, giving the elderly a chance to enjoy music they knew and for children to learn a different aspect of traditional popular music.

A past student, Ann Clewlow, comes from Weston-super-Mare for singing brush-ups while her husband Chris drives her the many miles to Hampshire. Ann has numerous individual students as well as being conductor of three choirs. I am so proud of her!

I had many pool parties for Alice, which went well until one day on a dark evening there was a sudden cry, "Wendy, a Chinaman has just fallen into the pool!" He turned out to be the father of one of Alice's Chinese friends.

My godson, Jonathan with me on Alice's Wedding Day

I have been totally spoilt for my birthdays. For my 70th Alice took me to New York with all its splendour. I decided from a young age that if I reached the age of 80, I would invite my friends and family to celebrate the occasion, never thinking that I would reach that age. Alice put on an incredible party with a cook at hand and where many of my past students were invited to sing if they felt so inclined, with the pianist Matthew Unsult from college to assist. They were all amazing and my godson, Jonathan, also sang. He writes his own music and has been travelling abroad to hear choirs performing his compositions. I sang a German Lied, not particularly well, but it was fun. Alice and Laurence joined me for a further celebration with professional musical friends and acquaintances we had known for many years, at the Festival Hall to dinner and a following concert. One comment from a friend was, "How wonderful to hear a concert without singers, Wendy!"

We heard Britten's *Violin Concerto* and Tchaikovsky's *5th Symphony* which he obviously enjoyed immensely as did we all.

Talking of my friends now I have been happily ensconced in Hampshire for almost twenty years and I do admit that I miss my friends in and around London, particularly my Academy friend, Josephine Rippon, and my godson, Jonathan Rippon. Last but not least my clever sister, born just one year before me, meaning we always wore closely identical clothes, with Harriet either keeping a keen watch on my behaviour, or with her head firmly in a book. Harriet and I were so different but enjoyed times together, especially with both having musical interests. She loved living in the bungalow in Four Lanes. She preferred not to visit London but we, conversely, loved to go back to Cornwall to stay for a few days with her. One thing we had in common was that we both loved Alice dearly. Alice was keen to play at Harriet's funeral, but, since all flights had been cancelled, she had, after her concerts, to race through Spain and France, running the gauntlet of traffic police, in a hired car in order to reach the funeral to play for her, with just minutes to spare.

Wendy's hat party with her friends

I will never forget some wonderful friends who have all passed away and were so much a large part of my life. Marie Hayward Segal, a Wagnerian singer who had sung a lot in Germany, and Pat Conti, who played the role of Abbess in the West End production of *The Sound of Music* and whom I had met at Glyndebourne. Wendy Smith, a Royal Academy of Music student, and Sally Le Sage, a soprano colleague. Margrit Kensbock, first met in London then later on the south coast, was a pianist who had been coached by Geoffrey. Sylvia Eaves I first met in *Robert and Elizabeth* and at Glyndebourne. Sylvia Rhys-Thomas I also met at Glyndebourne. Robert Aldwinkle I met in The Handel Opera Society and later at Trinity Laban Conservatoire of Music and Dance. There was Rear Admiral Tony Norman, husband of Judy Norman OBE, Winifred Johns, my flatmate when we were at the Academy, and the celebrated Cornish novelist and poet, D.M. Thomas.

After a musically eventful life, with much travelling throughout the world, Michael and I are now content to stay put in our cosy Victorian house, situated in the bustling market town of Lymington, Hampshire, where we are surrounded by the New Forest and not far from the sea, which I dearly love. From Milford-on-Sea the view across the Solent reminds me of happy childhood days on the beaches at Falmouth and St Ives. The sea vista past The Needles is always the same yet constantly changing, like life itself.

Wendy on a day out with her grandchildren

Alice and her family on holiday

Appendix

Rudimentary thoughts for female voices.

Every vowel and consonant has a unique position:
E's have two. A square, firm approach of the mouth (like a kiss). A straight position of the mouth (like a smile) above the special B♭ B or C depending on the tessitura of the voice. B♭ for a light soprano, B for a lyric soprano and C for a coloratura. Notes below a B♭ B or C to be sung with firm breath support which is always so important. The jaw is to be dropped.
For the position for Aws and Oos think of an Egg!

The jaw has three positions:
The largest open mouth drop for vowels Ah, Eh, I, Aws and Oos and for very important words in a phrase which have to be accentuated.
The smaller jaw drop is for the position used most of all, as in speech.
The smallest jaw drop is for insignificant words like *the, if, at, of* and *up.*
It is very difficult as a general rule to keep a jaw drop and for the smaller jaw drop, when above a B I practised this so much without singing that my cheek bones ached after a while.
The smallest jaw drop is below a B♭, B and C. It is advisable to use the body support for lower notes at the same time as a small smile using the largest jaw drop, particularly in sopranos where lower notes can be weaker.

When the placement of the voice is understood singing is such a joy but correct breath control has to underpin the whole process otherwise singing is hard work. Added to that, concentrating on the pronunciation of languages, dynamics, phrasing and dramatic input is of great importance.

www.ingramcontent.com/pod-product-compliance
Lightning Source LLC
Chambersburg PA
CBHW051209090426
42740CB00021B/3438